SIXTY-NINE
WAYS TO
START A
STUDY GROUP
—AND—
KEEP IT
GROWING

LAWRENCE O. RICHARDS

SIXTY-NINE WAYS TO START A STUDY GROUP
—AND—
KEEP IT GROWING

ZONDERVAN PUBLISHING HOUSE OF THE ZONDERVAN CORPORATION
GRAND RAPIDS, MICHIGAN 49506

69 WAYS TO START A STUDY GROUP AND KEEP IT GROWING
Copyright © 1973 by The Zondervan Corporation
Grand Rapids, Michigan

ISBN 0-310-31981-1
Revised edition 1980

Library of Congress Catalog Card Number 73-8443

Printed in the United States of America

83 84 85 86 87 88 — 10 9 8 7 6 5 4

contents

1

meeting for ministry

The Detroit lady was very positive. I was speaking to a Sunday school staff about the role of interpersonal relationships in teaching, and she was reacting. "That sounds like 'small group' talk. I'd rather hear a well-prepared teacher lecture. I've been in groups for the past four years, and it's just a sharing of ignorance."

I could sympathize with her feelings. I've been in groups that were disappointing, too. Groups that came together because some of us felt a need — yet groups that after some months left us all a little disappointed. Disappointed because we hadn't found that we were hoping for.

I've found that many groups Christians form turn out this way. They're formed in hope and expectation. But as the weeks go by, they bring a sense of disappointment. A sense of something missing.

Yet I've talked with other Christians who have experienced positive and exciting things in their groups. I've known the positive, too — times when God has met and significantly changed the lives of men and women through their involvement with small groups of other Christians. And my family now attends a church [1] actually built around the interaction of its members in "little churches" that meet during the week. For us, the dynamic of the little churches makes a constant impact on individual Christian experience and on the life of our church as a whole.

The conclusion I've come to over the years is simple. The small groups of Christians meeting together can succeed — or fail. There is no magic in the "small group" itself, but when in that smaller group we experience the meeting of the Body of Christ for ministry, exciting and positive things do happen!

Why a group?

The word "success" immediately suggests that a small group has a purpose, a goal, and that we can tell when we've been successful in reaching or moving toward it. A quick look at writings on the small group, however, gives a confusing picture. We soon discover that a "small group" can be formed for a number of purposes! There are action groups — groups assembled to work on a particular task. There are personal groups — groups that form to get to know others in depth. There are therapy groups — people who meet to discuss and deal with deep, personal problems. There are study groups that meet to talk about books they are reading. Home Bible classes that usually meet with an evangelistic purpose. Bible study groups that meet to learn more about what the Bible says. All these — and others — are "small groups." But what a

[1] You can read about our church in the book, *Brethren, Hang Loose,* by Robert C. Girard (Grand Rapids: Zondervan, 1972).

variety of purposes. And how different the criteria of success in each.

So it's important for us to understand the kind of small group this book is talking about. Not that there's anything wrong with small groups which meet for other purposes. There isn't. But in this book we'll be thinking about a special kind of small group. A group that meets for just the things I think most of us yearn for, which most of us attempt to find in small groups. The kind of small group I'm thinking of now is the one *meeting for ministry*.

Where is God going?

Somehow this is the kind of question we always have to ask before we can say, "Where are *we* going?" After all, Jesus is Lord; He sets the direction of life. So we want to approach everything in life by asking where Jesus is going and then set our direction by His.

When we ask, "Where is God going in the lives of believers?" we get some exciting answers from the Bible. Jesus first hints at it in the Sermon on the Mount. After telling those who would listen that their lives are to be marked by an aggressive love, even for their enemies (Matt. 5:38-44), Jesus explains that this is appropriate because God Himself treats all with love, and we are to "be sons of your Father who is in heaven" (5:45 RSV). Somehow, because we *are* God's own children, it is fitting that we "be perfect, even as your Father in heaven is perfect" (5:48 *Living Bible*).

At first it's a jolt, this idea that we are to bear the stamp of God and express Him in our lives with others. But the theme is repeated. Phillips beautifully renders Paul's thought that God has chosen us "to bear the family likeness of his Son, that he might be the eldest of a family of many brothers" (Rom. 8:29 *Phillips*). The resemblance is made possible because salvation brings more than forgiveness: it brings *life*. "You are sons of God now," Peter reminds us. "The live, permanent Word of the living God has given you his own indestructible heredity" (1 Peter 1:23 *Phillips*).

We do have new life.

God's life.

So in each of us God is moving in a distinct and unique direction. Where is God going with us? *He is in the process of forming Christ in our total personalities.* He is bringing us to the place of saying with Paul, "I live; yet not I, but Christ liveth in me, and the life which I now live in the flesh I live by the faith of the Son of God, who loved me, and gave himself for me" (Gal. 2:20).

We have to get this in perspective. God is *not* primarily concerned with what we *do;* God's first concern is who we *are*. For God knows, as the Bible testifies, that the more we are like Jesus in our attitudes and values and our character, the more our behavior will be like His. Christians reach out to touch people — people in need, people suffering injustice, people without Christ — when their hearts beat with Jesus' own love.

The more we are like Jesus, the more we will act like Him in our world.

It is from this concept of where God is going that we catch the goal of the small group. The kind of small group this book is about is a group that helps each member move toward God's goal for us of Christlikeness. It is a *growing* group: a group come together to help each member grow in the Lord and move toward his fullest potential as a Christian person. When this kind of group meets, it is meeting for ministry. It is meeting for the ministry of each person in the lives of the others, to build up each member in the faith and love that is in Christ Jesus.

But is a group necessary?

Can't Christians reach their potential without a small group experience?

This is a most deceiving question because we have to answer both yes and no. Yes, because a person does not have to be in a "small group" to grow. No, because it's clear from Scripture that no believer can reach his potential in Christ *alone*.

In the last hours before the crucifixion, Jesus placed great emphasis on togetherness for His disciples (John 13 - 17). Over and over the themes of love and unity recur, initiated by the "new commandment." *Love one another.*

Jesus defined the kind of love He meant quite clearly. Believers are to love "just as I have loved you" (see John 15:12). How did Jesus love? Totally. And by involvement. He left the safety and isolation of heaven and entered fully into our world and our experiences. He participated in the lives of those He loved and gave Himself fully. To love "just as" Jesus loved *must* involve us deeply with other persons.

Such involvement need not take place in the small group. But the small group has sprung to prominence today because so many of us have not been involved in others' lives! The impersonalization and depersonalization of our society has struck deeply into the life of the Church and robbed us of our heart and warmth. To love Jesus' way, we

11

The Relationship

My Present Experience

	Satisfactory	?			Unsatisfactory

1. Receiving (Rom. 14:1) — I know others who accept and value me as I am.

2. " — I freely accept and appreciate others, even when they seem "different" from me.

3. Provoke (encourage) (Heb. 10:24) — I have friends who encourage and stimulate me to keep on growing when I feel low.

4. " — I am being used to motivate others to fresh trust when they are discouraged.

5. Forgive (Eph. 4:32) — I freely confess faults to others.

6. " — I've found freedom to forgive others.

7. " — I am close to others who do ask forgiveness when they hurt me.

8. Bear burdens (Gal. 6:1) — I am praying for burdens others have shared with me.

9. " — I have recently shared my burdens and know others are praying for me.

10. Impact — I have a warm feeling that I'm not alone in the Christian life — I'm experiencing what it means to be one of many brothers.

have to really know and really care about one another as persons. It is precisely the awareness of lost contact with others that has led so many to join or form groups.

So the question, "Is the small group necessary?" is really the wrong one to ask. What each of us needs to ask instead is, "Do I need to be closer to other Christians than I am?" Or "Will meeting with a smaller group of Christians help me develop the dimension of love, and encourage my growth toward Christlikeness?"

How may we tell if a small group is something we need? One way is to check what the Bible tells us about the kinds of relationships that are to exist among Christians. If you or I have these relationships with others now, the chances are we do *not* need a small group. If we aren't experiencing these relationships with other believers, the right kind of small group can probably make a significant contribution to our own spiritual growth and to the meaningfulness of our Christian faith.

On page 12 are listed some of the dimensions of relationship the Bible speaks of. Why not check out your own life and decide if perhaps you need to become involved in the kind of group this book is about?

These are just some of the dimensions of relationship that the Bible speaks of as important to our spiritual health. These relationships do not have to happen in a small group — but they do have to happen! Meetings of the Church must have this interpersonal involvement dimension, as the writer to Hebrews stresses: "Let us think of one another and how we can encourage one another to love and do good deeds. And let us not hold aloof from our church meetings, as some do. Let us do all we can

13

to help one another's faith, and this the more earnestly as we see the day drawing ever nearer" (Heb. 10:24, 25 *Phillips*).

God knows that we need each other.

God has given us each other.

And we do have to draw near each other.

Questions

Many questions are raised about small groups. Some we may answer briefly because they aren't addressed to the central issues. Yet they are questions that bother people who are drawn to the group experience but feel hesitant.

How large is a small group? The size is open. It should be small enough so all may participate and really come to know each other significantly. Ten or so people is a good starter size.

Where does a small group meet? Usually in a home. The atmosphere of informality seems to help people open up.

Should a group be "closed" or open to anyone? It's probably not best to have a group "for members only." Other believers who want to come should be welcomed. If the group grows too large, it may be divided.

Should a group be age-graded? No. The main need is to have a unity of purpose and a desire to know Christ better. Differences in age and experience may help the group.

How long should a group stay together? There's no set rule. Sometimes it's good to start with a 10-week commitment. Then decide whether to go on for another three months or so. The main thing is to keep open as a group to God's leading, and let Him divide, stop, or restart the group as He wills.

How much time should a group meeting take? Always more than one hour, seldom as much as three. Many groups find that a two-hour limit helps keep their purposes in focus.

How often should a group meet? Most groups prefer weekly sessions.

Should non-Christians be invited? The purposes of this kind of group are not directly evangelistic. But as witnessing takes place, it's often appropriate to bring in the non-Christian who is seriously considering Christ. Indiscriminate invitations to non-Christians, though, will change the character of the group. Meeting for ministry is to build up believers so that evangelization will take place out in the world.

Does the small group replace the church? Not at all! The small group should never be viewed as a replacement for the congregational gathering. Nor is small group Bible study a substitute for preaching of the Word. The healthy church has *both* the small-group-type activity and a strong corporate ministry of worship and Bible teaching.

What about leaders? Any group will have leaders. The question is what *kind* of leaders? Some leaders are viewed as those who "control" meetings, others as those who provide dynamic examples of Christian living. You do not need the control-type leader for a small group, instead, use the studies provided in this and similar helps to give the group initial direction. But you *do* need people who will set the pace in openness, in sharing, in honesty, in commitment, and in dedication to Christ and one another.

15

What else do we need?

So far, in this introductory chapter, I've suggested that a small group *meeting for ministry* (to build each other up and help each other move toward God's goal of Christlikeness) can make an important contribution to any believer's life. While it is not necessary for such ministry to have "small groups," a Christian may find a small group a definite help if he does not yet have the kind of relationships with other believers that the Bible says are to mark the Body of Christ. This is really a personal decision. Each of us has to look at his own life and evaluate. Do I need to draw closer to others than I am? If so, a small group may help.

What do we need to make our small group experience a healthy one? to actually experience the ministry and growing that God intends for us? *That's what the rest of this book is about.*

From this point we go on to explore five critical elements in the life of a group that is meeting for ministry: Identification, Affirmation, Exploration, Concentration, Adoration. Each element is explored in a chapter of its own. With each discussion, you're given (1) a complete session plan that you may use in a small group to help the group experience this element, and learn by experience what is involved, and (2) a number of *activity ideas.* Each of the activity ideas is designed to help strengthen your group's experience of a particular element and may be used when a group feels the element is missing or given insufficient emphasis.

Help, not an answer

In the last analysis, though, we have to guard against the feeling that this book, or any other, gives The Answer. There is no magic formula, no process that "always works." The life of any group that comes together for ministry is a complex mix of personalities — and a unique process guided and influenced by the Holy Spirit. At best a book like this can give insight into how the Holy Spirit wants to work in the fellowship of believers — and at best, you and I in our groups can determine to open our lives to Him and to His working. Resting in God's love, confident that God's purposes for us are good, we can move into the small group as into any new experience, trusting God to shape and to guide all that we commit fully to Him.

ACTION IDEAS

1. How may you discover others who sense the same need for fellowship and meeting for ministry that you feel? Ask your pastor to put this or a similar notice in the church bulletin, to be deposited in the offering plate by any interested.

   FELLOWSHIP!

   If you feel a need for a deeper relationship with other Christians, and for help in deepening your own relationship with the Lord, you may want to *meet for ministry* with others who feel the same. Just fill out the following, and deposit it in the offering plate, or mail to the church this week.

   Name _____ Age ____

   Address _____

   Phone _____

   Contact those who respond and set up a time to meet and talk about forming a group. One way to prepare them for such a meeting is to ask each to read the first chapter of this book to gain insight into the possible purposes of a small group fellowship.

2. Often the start of a ministry group is rather slow. It takes a while to get to know others and to learn how to interact. Thus, many like to get a group started on a Friday-Saturday retreat. This added time does encourage development of greater depth of relationships and development of study skills.

   What should you do on a launching retreat? Provide for fun times as well as study times! And for the group times, you might

   a. Use one of the two retreat plans in this book (pp. 108, 126), or ideas from the ACTION IDEAS section in chapters 2 through 5.

   b. Use a book like Lyman Coleman's *Serendipity* study, "Breaking Free" (Word Books).

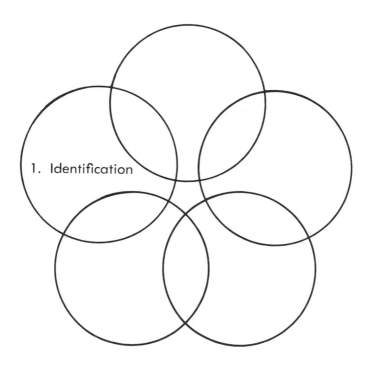

Essential Elements

1. Identification

2

identification

Three people dropped in to tell me about a new church they've formed. They were excited about what God is doing . . . but troubled because of one dimension they feel has been missing. Fellowship.

Most of us feel a need for fellowship. Oh, not the superficial friendliness that sometimes passes for fellowship, but the deeper relationship that develops when Christians sense with others that somehow they are *together* in this business of living the Christian life.

The New Testament word for fellowship, *koinonia,* communicates the deepest kind of togetherness. It's a togetherness that has all things in common, that shares the most intimate things of life, from agonies to joys. The Apostle John expresses it beautifully: "We want you to be with us in this — in this fellowship with the Father, and Jesus Christ his Son" (1 John 1:3 *Phillips*). How exciting to realize that we never have to feel *alone* in our experience of the Christian life. God has given us others to be *with us* in a growing fellowship relationship with Jesus.

Yet so many Christians these days do feel alone. They struggle to trust God more, they fail and feel guilty, and so often they never realize that others around them have the same experiences. They never realize that God has placed us together so we might support and help each other as we share experiences common to us all.

Often this is particularly hard to realize — that others *are* like us. That the problems and frustrations we feel are experienced by others, too. That there is no test or temptation that has gripped us which is not "common to man" — and that God has made a way to escape so we might bear our burdens and overcome (1 Cor. 10:13). As human beings we experience those things that *are* "common to man." We do have an identity with other people. And for a group that meets for ministry, in order to minister we must experience our identity with others.

Our identity with every man

Actually, we may establish identity with other people because, first of all, we have our humanity in common.

It's important to start here. Even before a person is a Christian, there is an identity we share with him. And after we come to possess God's gift of new life? We retain that identity.

Jan was brought up in a home where her father worried that she might become vain and frivolous. So he was careful to guard against any possible budding pride or apparent interest in herself. If he saw her glance in a mirror to fix her hair, he'd say, "You don't have to look in a mirror to see if you're beautiful. I'll tell you when you're beautiful." And he never told her.

Jan and her father illustrate two things it means to be human beings. Jan was vulnerable. She could be hurt, and she was. Her father's approach to life crushed her, making her feel worthless and unhappy. No wonder that as an adult Jan has had a hard time accepting herself or accepting the fact that life for a Christian can be a truly new and different thing. She still hears overtones of her father's voice when she reads the Bible, and she finds it hard to believe that God is saying, "You *are* beautiful. I love you: you are fully accepted in the beloved" (see Eph. 1:6).

Jan's father? He was mistaken. He was wrong. Whatever his motives (they may have been good, or deep down there may have been a twisted motive flowing from the sin that is seated in all of our personalities), he hurt his daughter. And we're all like this. We have the capacity to hurt others. We lack the wisdom to do good. We may be mistaken and wrong. As human beings, all of us are so limited, so far from all we want to be.

We sometimes think of "sin" only as the strong, wrong impulses that we feel. But there is far more to being a sinner than that. Biblically, sin means that our personalities are warped out of God's intended shape; that our limitations rise up and overcome us, so that even when we *want* to do good, we lack the power. Romans puts it this way: "I don't accomplish the good I set out to do, and the evil I don't really want to do I find I am always doing" (see 7:15). No wonder Paul complains about "the sin which has made its home within me!"

So don't fall into the trap of thinking that people who don't know Christ are radically different from you. They're different in only one way. They lack the life of God that comes through Jesus Christ. But in their humanity they are like you, and you

23

are like them. In our humanity, you and I are identified with every man.

Establishing our human identity

It's such a peculiar thing. You and I know from our own experience how real our identity as human beings is. I know how vulnerable I am. I know how foolishly and wrongly I often act, and how easily and lightly I hurt others. I set out to do good and end up doing harm. And you know you do the same. Yet none of us wants to admit this to others. We all want to appear strong, not weak.

Sometimes Christians even use their faith as an excuse for failing to be honest with each other. "I'm a Christian now," we argue with ourselves. "I'm supposed to overcome these things. I'd better not let others know what I'm really like, or they won't think I'm much of a Christian!" Even Christ is made to serve our pride.

There are several things wrong with this approach to the Christian life. Several things that are destructive to our relationships with other believers.

It denies the Gospel. That's right. The failure to accept and affirm our identity as human beings does deny the Gospel. The Gospel is that Jesus died for sinners (not for the "strong"). The Bible says, "when we were yet without strength, . . . Christ died for the ungodly" (Rom. 5:6). *And we never get over being the ungodly.* We never become the strong. Jesus underlines this fact when He says, "apart from me you can do nothing" (John 15:5 RSV).

The Gospel is a truly unique thing. It is God's promise to give us life and then to live that life in us. It is God's promise that when we accept our weakness and inadequacy, He will provide His supernatural power and His vitality, and He will come alive in us. *This* is the Gospel. And it's such good news!

So we can see how pretending that we're strong is to deny the Gospel. When we pretend to be something we aren't, we rob God of the glory that is His alone for the growth and change that is taking place in our personalities. The Apostle Paul realized this, and he came to view his weaknesses (including physical disabilities) as an opportunity for God to show His power more completely. His weaknesses meant "a deeper experience of the power of Christ" (cf. 2 Cor. 12:1-11).

When I am willing to reveal my weaknesses to others, *then* they may see the power of Christ as He works to overcome them. Then I *demonstrate* — not deny — the Gospel.

It cuts us off from others. Feeling that we have to hide our real selves from other people puts a terrible burden on us. We're forced to wear a mask all the time. The longer we try to fake it, the deeper grows the fear that sometime we'll let the mask slip. So we tend to draw away from people; we feel uncomfortable when we come close, and are vulnerable to discovery.

Then we're truly alone.

It's such a terrible, empty thing to be alone.

Something inside us seems to die.

It cuts others off from help. So many Christians these days are looking for help and encouragement. They realize their inadequacies all too well and long for hope.

Bryan was a leader in his church. A layman, he led the song services, often preached when the pastor was on vacation or out of town, and was always the first on his feet to give a testimony. He was the picture of a strong, vital, victorious Christian.

So he couldn't understand it when Doug and Fran, a young couple who had recently been converted, left the church and, when asked why, cited Bryan as the reason. When he visited them he was jolted by their explanation. "Well," Doug told him, "week after week we saw how happy you were and heard you tell of all the great things God was doing through you. But we're *not* happy. We're having an awful lot of problems being Christians. We finally decided we could just never be like you. So we quit."

Doug and Fran knew their own inadequacy too well, *and they could not identify with a person who seemed so unlike them.*

There's a biblical principle that explains what happened here — and what has to happen if we are to establish identity with one another. It's found in 2 Corinthians 1, nestled in a description of God as One who

> comforts us in all our affliction, so that we may be able to comfort those who are in any affliction, with the comfort with which we ourselves are comforted by God. . . . If we are afflicted, it is for your comfort and salvation; and if we are comforted, it is for your comfort. . . . Our hope for you is unshaken; for we know that as you share in our sufferings, you will also share in our comfort.
>
> (vv. 4, 6, 7 RSV)

The apostle immediately goes on to share about "the affliction we experienced in Asia; for we were so utterly, unbearably crushed that we despaired of life itself" (2 Cor. 1:8-11 RSV). Paul ministered as a needy human being to other needy human beings — not as the strong to the weak.

We can see here a distinct progression of thought and experience.

— we suffer affliction
— God comforts (encourages) us
— others suffer afflictions
— we share God's comfort with them

It is because we know what it means to be human and in need, and because we have known the touch of God, that we may bring comfort to others who will identify with us. Have you known despair? Then share it, so others may see that you are real and see in you the reality of God.

To communicate the reality of God we must share our humanness . . . that inadequacy of ours which made us NEED Him.

This is what Doug and Fran struggled with. They simply could not identify with Bryan. He spoke of the great things God was doing — but never shared his sense of need for God. He never revealed to them the fact that he was like them in his humanity.

A dual identity

Understanding something about identification helps us see what should be happening in a group that meets for ministry. We meet for fellowship — for the encouragement that comes when we realize that we are "in this" together with others. For this kind of fellowship, identity needs to be established on two levels.

We need to experience our identity as inadequate and human.

We need to experience our identity as Christ's persons, in whom Jesus lives and is working.

27

This is what sets the Christian apart. Not that he is "different from" others, but that, while he is the same, Christ has been added! Jesus has come into the believer's personality through faith, and Jesus Himself lives in him. Figure 1 shows one way we may visualize the relationship between these two identities of ours.

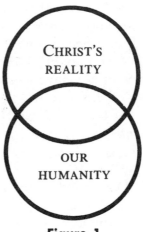

Figure 1
Our dual identity

Each Christian is a human being, bearing all the limitations of a fallen human nature. But each believer *also* has been given the gift of Christ's life. Jesus Himself has entered, and He is with us to live out His own life through us.

In a very real way we can say God's goal for the Christian is that more and more these two circles might overlap. Not that we should be less human, but that more and more Christ's adequacy might be experienced in overcoming our inadequacies. The goal of a group that meets for ministry: to encourage and stimulate this process of experiencing Christ's life!

Figure 2
Our goal: toward a
fuller experience
of Christ

To encourage movement toward this goal effectively, it is important that the members of a ministry group *establish identity with each other on both these levels!*

We need to know each other in our humanity. We need to know each other as persons in whom Jesus lives.

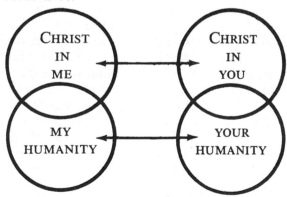

Figure 3
We need to know each
other in both identities

Why some groups fail

The principle I've just stated ("Members of a ministry group need to establish identity with each other on both levels.") is a vital one. It helps us understand why some groups have been deeply disappointing to their members.

(1) *Facades.* Sometimes groups form to "study the Bible" but talk about it only in generalities or as ideas. The people in these groups fail to share on *either* level. Any hurts they feel are bottled up inside and continue to ache. Any exciting touches of God's hand are held back because sharing them might seem to be pride. In this setting no fellowship is experienced, and the members' lives generally remain untouched.

(2) *Phonies.* Sometimes groups develop the habit of sharing only the positive experiences. "I witnessed to three people this week." "The Lord answered our prayers for the fourth week in a row!" "I've felt so *good* all week." When this pattern is established, some who may have deep needs, or even passing problems, hesitate to share them. The others seem so strong there is the fear they might not understand. Or the fear that the others would look down on them as "less spiritual." This pattern denies the fact that we are human beings and that we are all subject to failure, frustration, pressures, and sins. Over a period of time, as our humanness is increasingly hidden, the group experience becomes more and more unreal. The phoniness and hypocrisy of the members destroy relationships, and the group dies.

(3) *Failures.* Other groups begin by exploring their needs and problems in depth. These groups may very quickly establish a sense of identity as human beings, and they often develop a healthy

30

openness and honesty. But it is easy for such groups to limit sharing to the problem, or failure, level. At first, in such a group, there is a sense of release and progress. Just finding others with whom to share brings a sense of relief. But over a period of weeks or months, the feeling of progress fades, and each meeting the same old problems are hashed over again and again. Lu and Carl had another fight . . . and so we go over their grievances again and probe and question and try to provide insight and advice. But we know that soon they'll fight again, and we'll talk it all over again. There's no *change* taking place in the group members.

Once this climate is established, such a group will often resist attempts to move toward the level of seeking identification as people in whom Christ lives. They have been trapped in a static relationship.

Static and dynamic

The group that meets for ministry seeks a dynamic experience of Jesus Christ. It's important to realize that while we must establish our identity as human beings with other members of the group, the primary reason for establishing identity on this level is to enable us to see the reality of Christ at work in our personalities.

If we can establish identity only on the human level, we set up a static situation that is destined to disappoint. *We can not grow out of ourselves as human beings.* We change only as we release more of ourselves to Christ's control, as we learn to trust ourselves more fully to Him.

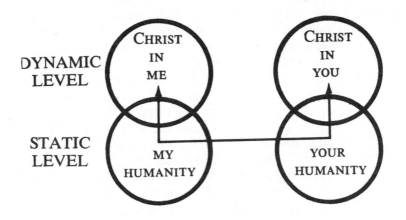

Figure 4

To establish our identity with others, we need to see them first as human beings, that we might then see them as persons in whom Christ is a living reality.

Our goal, then, is to come to know each other and experience our identity both as human beings and as persons in whom Christ is a living reality. We want to see each other in our inadequacies, that we might see Christ at work in us. We share our needs and our problems, but we never *stop* there (in a static relationship). We go on to share how we are experiencing Jesus Christ in our lives. It is Christ who provides the dynamic for the small group. Seeing Jesus in others, we find hope and are freed to trust Him more.

When we have this kind of relationship with other Christians, our fellowship with Christ grows, too. The Bible tells us that the Holy Spirit works through members of the Body of Christ to build up each individual part (Eph. 4:11-13).

Where there is *this kind of fellowship,* growth *will* take place.

The role of the model

Why does it work this way? Why do we need each other? The only answer we can give is, really, God planned it thus. He formed us into one Body. He made us brothers and sisters with a need for a family relationship. He gave each of us spiritual gifts to use in ministering to each other.

Particularly, God created us in such a way that we need models. We need to *see* in an example the reality of His words. We see this thought reflected throughout the Bible. "Let me be your example in this," Paul says a number of times. And to one church, "what you have . . . heard and seen in me, do; and the God of peace will be with you" (Phil. 9:4 RSV). To Timothy he recalls the years together and the fact that the young man has thoroughly known both his teachings and his manner of life (2 Tim. 3:10); he warns Timothy to pay attention to his life and his teaching.

When elders are to be chosen, the church is told to select men whose lives exemplify the working of God in them. Peter reminds his fellow elders that they are not to act like little tin gods, but to serve as examples for the flock (1 Peter 5:1-5).

It's the same in the Old Testament. How significant that parents are told first to have God's words in their own hearts and then to teach them diligently to their children (Deut. 6:1-6). Children need to see in their parents' lives the reality of the words their parents speak.

33

And finally, of course, there is God's own example. When it came time to communicate Himself fully, He did it in a flesh-and-blood way. He became a man. In the person of Jesus Christ, we may *see* the Father.

Each of us needs models.

Each of us needs to see the reality in others' lives.

The small town where I'm from in Michigan sprawls out around a little lake. In the fall, when it freezes over, you can always see along the shore line broken limbs and rocks that have been thrown out onto the ice and have broken through. Kids like me did it — youngsters who went down to the lake when it began to freeze and wanted to see if the ice were safe for skating. We would find something heavy to throw out first to see if the ice would break.

Just imagine you're standing there now, looking out on the ice, wondering. Along comes someone else. He's read the temperatures down at the bank on Main street, and he's sure it's safe. So he tells you, "Go on out. It's safe. I know it's safe."

But still you hesitate. Maybe you put your foot out tentatively — and pull back as you hear the creak and moan that always marks the early ice along a shore. He's told you it's safe — but you hesitate.

Now imagine that your friend, carrying his skates, walks out onto the ice right in front of you. Turning, he looks back at you and smiles. "Come on out. See? It's safe. It holds me!"

This is what we're looking for — and what we can find — in a fellowship of believers who meet for ministry. How rich an encouragement it is when we know others *like us* who have stopped telling us

34

to go . . . and who step out in front, inviting us to *come.*

ACTION IDEAS

Here are some things you may do in a small group to get to know each other better. Some of them encourage sharing on the level of our common humanity; others stress our experience with Christ. Some encourage sharing on both levels. Use them when starting a group or when you feel your sense of identity with each other is slipping. (The numbering continues from the ACTION IDEAS on page 18.)

3. *What has my life been like?*
   Graph your spiritual experience.

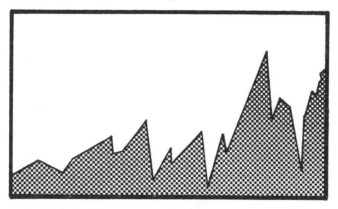

Many Christians find their lives marked by ups and downs. Give each member of the group paper and crayon, and ask each to graph the peaks and valleys of his life.

Variations. Make the graph represent the whole life, before and after conversion. Or make the graph represent only experience as a Christian. The pattern may be then shared with and explained to the group by each member.

For greater depth. Have members specifically label each peak and valley (or the most significant ones). Discuss these in greater depth as all seek to understand one another better.

4. *Where am I now?*

Explain the two circles used in the chapter to illustrate our dual identity (pages 28, 29). Ask each person to draw two circles representing himself, indicating where he feels he is right now in terms of experiencing Christ's adequacy.

For instance, one might feel he is a long way from knowing the meaning of Christ in his life and thus draw the circles as barely touching.

Another might feel more encouraged and draw considerable overlap.

After each person has drawn his own diagram, he explains what he has drawn and why he feels this portrays him just now. The group is free to interact with the one who is sharing and may share in return.

5. *Are others really like me?*

Give paper and pen to each group member and ask him to take five to eight minutes to describe an experience or situation that made an impact on who he is as a person — but which he has felt was so unusual that few could understand or identify with it. After the descriptions have been written, have each person list on the back of the paper the feelings he associates with the experience.

Then have individuals read their descriptions. After each is read, other members of the group should say what feelings they believe are associated with that experience. The one who read then reports the feelings he has listed on the

36

back of his paper and explains them. *For greater depth:* following each person's sharing, have other group members tell of times when they felt like the reader.

6. *How do I experience Christ?*

Have each member of the group jot down quickly five times when Jesus seemed very real and close to him. Go around the group, sharing the five. As each person shares his list, the group members should look for a pattern. For instance, one person might list instances of sorrow or tragedy. Group members might note this and suggest, "You seem to see Jesus as someone very warm and loving, and look to Him for comfort." Or "You really must trust Him a lot. When things like that happen to me, I get mad. But you still sense His love."

Another group member might list instances of recovery after failures or sins. Group members would note for him, "You seem to see Jesus as a real overcomer, someone who turns your life around."

It's exciting to realize that Jesus can and does meet all our needs. This kind of sharing should help the group see the Lord's adequacy in a fresh way, and develop identity with others as those who share Christ's life too.

7. *Quickie re-entry activities*

Sometimes a short time of sharing at the beginning of a group session will re-establish or remind of identity already established. Here are several incomplete sentences group members may be invited to complete with the first thought that comes to mind. Start off a group session with these, using one to three per session.

(a) One word that describes my week is . . .
(b) Right now I feel . . .

(c) To me Jesus is like . . .

(d) I'm happy about . . .

(e) I'm sad about . . .

(f) One thing I really like about myself today is . . .

(g) One thing I don't like about myself today is . . .

(h) I'm thankful that . . .

(i) Life gets _____ all the time.

(j) What I want most from life right now is . . .

(k) One thing I enjoyed doing this week was . . .

(l) One thing I did today because I had to was . . .

(m) Today what I'd like to change about myself is . . .

(n) The biggest evidence that Jesus is in me now is . . .

(o) I feel like (select an animal or bird and tell why) . . .

SESSION PLAN

The Bible study on pages 112-17 is designed to help the group develop a sense of identity.

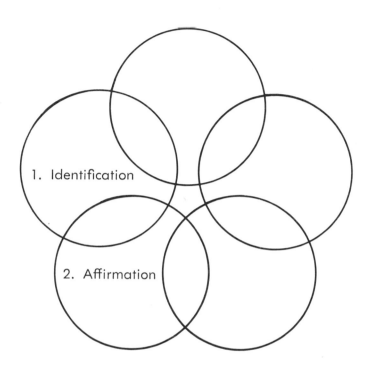

1. Identification

2. Affirmation

Essential Elements

1. Identification
2. Affirmation

3

affirmation

Mal is the youngest member of a small group that began meeting recently. At the first meeting all the members graphed their lives to date (see ACTION IDEA 3, p. 35), and Mal was the second to share. His story was unique, yet all too common.

Mal was born totally deaf. For eight years he could neither hear nor speak. Then he was fitted with hearing aids, and it was at this point that his life really began. He went to school and though learning was a problem, he did learn. He finished high school and went on to college. There he became a Christian, and there, in the early months of his life in Christ, his life peaked. He had been lonely before: uncertain in his relationships with others.

Now Mal threw himself into Campus Crusade evangelism and saw others profess Christ through his witness. He studied the Bible for hours, struggling with still nagging intellectual questions. But, despite all his activities, Mal still felt lonely. He looked at other Christians who seemed to be experiencing such abundance in their lives; he compared the emptiness he felt, emptiness that no amount of activity seemed to fill. His life seemed to drop steeply from the peaks to a dreadful, deep valley.

As Mal shared with the group his purpose for coming, he said simply that he wanted to see God's Word come alive as a reality to him instead of it being an intellectual exercise. He couldn't understand why he was still lonely, why he couldn't seem to find a job, why all his time spent in Bible study and witnessing didn't deserve better results than he seemed to get from God.

A unique experience? Yes, in many ways. How few of us are born deaf and live with deficient communication for nearly a decade of our lives! How few of us have such a traumatic adjustment in trying to learn to relate to other people!

And yet, as Mal shared, it became clear that in so many ways he was just like the rest of us. So many of us have thrown ourselves into service as a way to prove to ourselves that we really are worthwhile. So many have looked at others and wondered why things seem to go so well for them and not for us. So many have felt and do feel loneliness and doubt.

As the group talked on that evening, one of the members put his hand on Mal's arm and said, "Mal, I hope one thing that comes to you through our meeting together is the awareness that God loves *you* — that *you* are important to Him, totally apart from what you can do for Him." Mal smiled and said, "I know what you mean. I was talking to our pastor this morning, and that's what he said I needed, too. Just to realize that God really loves me."

To realize

It's so hard for many of us. Larry was in a group studying Genesis 2 and looking at all the ways God showed Adam he was important to Him. As the group talked about what it means to be made "in the image of God" (Gen. 1:26, 27), Larry said it made him feel frightened and uneasy. "It's such a responsibility. There are such high standards I have to live up to if I'm supposed to be like Him. I don't feel comfortable with the idea at all!"

Was Larry's reaction understandable? It was totally understandable from a person who had not fully realized that God loves us *as we are* (Rom. 5:8) and that each person is valuable and important to Him.

This is hard for many of us to accept.

Me?

Important to God?

Valuable?

Worthwhile?

Am I worth loving *as I am?* How can I be, when all my experiences have shown me that others value me for what I do? My parents show they love me when I do what they expect. People at church accept me only when I live up to their standards. People I work with like me only when I fit in. My employer values me only when I do my job. When our experiences of life are like this, how can *we* be worth loving? How can we be worth loving when we have to struggle so hard to be accepted and when we feel so guilty and ashamed at falling short?

How can we be worth loving when we *do* fall short — over and over again — in marriage, as

43

parents, as neighbors, in our work, in our struggles to become the kind of person we really want to be? How can we be worth loving *as we are?*

Feelings like these, common to Mal and Larry alike, keep us from accepting the fact that God does love and value us. Feelings like these keep us from finding the freedom both to love ourselves and to love Him.

Psychologists have a term for a person who feels unhappy about himself. They say he has a "low self-image." Somehow he can't bring himself to accept or to like himself. And they also point out that a low self-image tends to dominate and determine a person's responses to life. A person will act in a way consistent with his picture of himself.

Carol has learned to view herself as fat and weak. When she starts one of her many new diets, she starts almost in despair. She'll try it. But she sees herself as a fat person. A weak person. And, sure enough, she loses control on the third day and goes over her limit. Ashamed and guilty and angry with herself, she goes on an eating binge. In self-hate she thinks, "See? I knew I'm no good! I'm just weak and fat . . . and I'll always be fat."

Carol acted in a way which confirmed her picture of herself. Though consciously she didn't want to, she still had to prove to herself that she really is the kind of person she thinks she is.

Some try desperately to prove they are *not* the kind of persons they think they are. This desire seems to have been partly at the root of Mal's active efforts in evangelism and Bible study: "I'll prove I'm valuable by what I do. I'll show myself I'm worth loving by accomplishing great things."

But even accomplishing much — Mal has probably won more people to Christ at 26 than you

44

or I ever will — didn't meet his deepest needs. He still felt alone. He still felt unloved — and unlovely. Mal still couldn't accept himself *as he is.*

Who are we?

This is a basic question each of us has to answer. Who am I? *Am* I important? Is my picture of myself and my evaluation of my worth an accurate one? Or am I living in a world of illusion?

It is here that God speaks to us with a striking message Bible-believing Christians often overlook and sometimes distort. *Each person is important.*

We hear the message first in creation. After God made all things and looked at each day's work, and pronounced it "good," He made man. Genesis says something about the creation of man that is said of no other living thing. "Let us make man in our image," God said, "after our likeness: and let them have dominion over the fish of the sea, and over the fowl of the air, and over the cattle, and over all the earth, and over every creeping thing that creepeth upon the earth. So God created man in his own image, in the image of God created he him, male and female created he them" (Gen. 1:26, 27).

God made man in His likeness.

Man alone.

So man is special.

And looking over that day's work, the Bible records God's evaluation: "it was *very* good" (1:31).

An objection is often raised at this point. Yes, Adam was "in God's image," but then sin entered. Man is to be seen now as a sinner. *Our awareness of ourselves as sinful is to dominate in our self-image!* The "likeness" has been lost!

45

But has it? There are answers to this objection.

(1) Men still bear the "image of God." Genesis 9:6 gives as a reason for capital punishment of a murderer the fact that God made man in His image. Man's specialness is so significant that even in a society of sinners it must be affirmed in the most jolting way. One who dares to strike down a human being — a person who is created special to God — must himself be struck down. And so God affirms the value of even fallen, sinful man.

This same thought is repeated in James 3:9, which plainly states that men "are made in the likeness of God" (RSV). Sin has distorted humanity from the pattern of the original creation and has marred the image. But the image is not lost. Each person is still special to God; each person still bears the likeness of the Eternal.

(2) "Image of God" is not, as some have thought, a synonym for holy. Holiness is one of the characteristics of God, yes. But He is a holy *Person*. It is the fact that God is personal — with all the capacities of a person for knowing and feeling and valuing and interacting and doing — that is central to our image of God. In the fact that human beings are also persons they are set apart from all the rest of creation. We are like God in our personhood.

Our characteristics differ — it is true. He is holy, we are not. He is love, and we can love — but we can also be mean and spiteful. And yet, in the fact of being persons, we are like Him . . . because we're persons, we're special. He made us special, and we remain special to Him.

We hear the same message in the Law. The message of the Bible that human beings are special and valued by God is, surprisingly, heard in the giving of Law as well as in the Creation. So many with a low self-image hear the standards of God as crushing and condemning, because they view standards as responsibilities they should live up to but cannot. How exciting to realize that, while Law is meant to crush the individual who tries to be good enough to earn God's favor (Rom. 3:19, 20), the giving of Law was an act of love. It affirmed man's specialness and value.

Deuteronomy puts it this way: "The Lord commanded us to do all these statutes . . . for our good always" (6:24). Law was not meant to be a way for the believer to "earn points" with God! Law was given as an expression of love, to help the believer live a happy, meaningful life — a life that is always in touch with reality, leading to ever fuller experiences of the love of God.

In giving standards, God was not shouting demands but showing us once again, "You are special to me."

We see the message most clearly in Christ. It is in Jesus that we encounter the depths of God's love for us. How important are we? How valuable? The gospel answer comes clearly: *"You are important enough for Me to die for!"*

When we hear this message, we simply have to stop and wonder. God knows our every inadequacy. He knows the sin that has woven tangled webs throughout our personalities. He knows the way we fail. He knows the lies we tell Him, and ourselves, to try to hide our motives. He knows us as we really are.

And still He loves us.

He did not spare His own Son, but freely gave Him up for us all (Rom. 8:32).

Am I valuable?

Am I worthwhile? As I am?

Every word and every act of God in Jesus Christ says *"Yes!* You are special to Me!"

Special enough for God to give His very best.

So it's here that we gain perspective on the balance we must strike between seeing ourselves as sinners and seeing ourselves in our essential worthwhileness and value. The fact that I am a sinner is not my *primary* identity. My primary identity is as a human being. As a human being I am created in the image of God, the object of the love of God, my worth measured only by the value one can set on the death of the only Son of God. *I am loved. As I am.*

The fact that I am a sinner is a part of my *secondary* identity. It is not *essential* to who I am, because, through the death of Christ, sin has been dealt with. I will not always be a sinner! Christ's death stripped away that fixedness and, while He is even now untangling the webs that block me from becoming all I can be in Him, I look forward to an eternity of total freedom from sin. And when sin is stripped completely away? I will still be me! A person. An individual. The *same* person. I will still be a unique human being whom God loved so much that He was willing to die to free me from something that doesn't have to be.

So you and I need to learn to see ourselves as God sees us. We need to distinguish between our primary identity (that which we are now and always will be, individuals created in the image of God and thus intrinsically valuable) and our secondary identity (that which has become a part of us, but which Christ's cross has destroyed and which His life is even now pushing out of our lives). When we learn how important we are to God, then we may begin to be important to ourselves. When we see how much God loves us, then we can begin to realize that we are actually to love ourselves!

Affirmation

Affirmation is what happens when you and I see each other as valuable and worthwhile, when we communicate this perception to each other.

Affirmation is simply communicating to another person, "You are important. You are loved."

Terri was in a small group of women who met mornings for ten weeks. It was an exciting experience! Each week the women studied and paraphrased a passage of Scripture, looking for ways to apply it. They told what they had been discovering and how they had responded to the Word during the week. Each prayed daily for all the others, focusing on a specific prayer request each presented weekly. And they saw their prayers being answered! There was such a sense of reality, of vitality. Each felt free to express her needs and her problems, to be real with each other. And each person knew she was loved and accepted by the others.

Later another group formed. There was the same number of women — ten. They met for the same length of time. But these women were afraid to share. They talked about the Bible but hid their lives. Telling about it, Terri commented, "There never was such a bunch of women with perfect marriages, wonderful children, and absolutely joyous Christian lives, with nothing that needed being prayed for. And there never was a more meaningless group!"

Terri meant, of course, that she was experiencing a phony group (see page 30). Here were women who would not reveal their humanity. They thus never came to see the reality of Jesus working in their lives.

Such groups happen, and they are most likely to happen when their members fail to realize that they can be loved *as they are.* They hide their real selves because they can't bring themselves to agree with God that they are valuable and worthwhile apart from anything they do.

Mal was this way. He had to try to do things to gain a sense of worth in accomplishment.

But this approach to life is tragically self-defeating. When we hide our real selves from others, we cut ourselves off from the fellowship we need to grow as Christians and as persons. When we try to earn God's approval, we put our relationship with Him on a works basis and cut ourselves off from the experience of His presence and power (Gal. 5:4). What each of us needs to learn is that we are to accept ourselves as we are, realize that God loves us *now,* and simply open up our lives to Him, to do in us what He wills.

But how do we learn to accept and love ourselves? How do we develop a better self-image?

We know we weren't born with an image of ourselves as "good" or "bad," as "valuable" or "worthless." This image developed over the years of our growing up, and it developed as we discovered how others saw us. If we had parents like those of Jan (page 22), the chances are we began to question our worth and value. Their attempts to keep us from being proud and self-confident succeeded only too well!

Sometimes a child may have parents who set unreasonably high expectations for him to fulfill. A dad who made Phi Beta Kappa insists his son try to match his grades. An athletic older brother sets standards a younger, less talented boy feels he has to live up to — but never can. A mother whose singing career is cut short by marriage wants her daughter to sing concert music, even though she simply doesn't have the voice. A girl who is plain wants desperately to be like attractive big sister. Often when such a child doesn't measure up, he feels it's his fault. That somehow, if he were only *better,* he'd be able to please Mom or Dad or himself. And so he, too, begins to doubt his worth and value.

We may say to such a person, "Listen! That image of yourself that's developed over the years . . . that's not the real *you.* You're not worthless! You're really important, someone worth loving." We may even say this on the authority of Scripture: "God loves you. *That's* how important you are!"

But the words alone simply do not change something that took root over so many, many years of experiences with people.

Can our self-image be changed? Really, it takes the power of God, working His own supernatural transformation by the Holy Spirit. But you and I may be used by God in another person's life as a channel through which the Spirit moves! An important element of the life of a group that meets for ministry is to be so used in each other's lives. One of the most important things we may do is to affirm one another: to say and demonstrate to each other that we are loved — as we are.

As a person experiences being loved and valued, God brings the truth of His words to life, and that person can change.

In our small groups we can come to know each other as we are and, knowing each other this way, show compellingly that, *as we are,* we are loved and valued.

Communicating love

The Bible gives us deep insights into how we may communicate this kind of love and valuing that we call affirmation. We see the importance of affirming in Jesus' "new" command: "A new commandment I give to you, that you love one another; even as I have loved you, that you also love one another" (John 13:34 RSV). *Just as* Jesus loves. Valuing for who we are — human beings, special to God — not valuing for what we do.

A look at the New Testament contexts in which relationships between "one another" are described gives us insight into how to express and communicate this kind of affirming love.

Welcome one another (Rom. 15:7). Recently a couple told me of their experience in a local church in Phoenix, Arizona. They were struck by the friendliness the first day they visited; several couples came up, introduced themselves, and said how glad they were to see the new folks. So the couple returned, and again they were met by other couples and welcomed warmly. But after six weeks they suddenly realized that while people kept saying "hello," they didn't *know* anyone there. And when they realized that all the people who had been so eager to meet them were "greeters" *assigned* to be friendly that day, they felt betrayed!

This isn't what the word translated "welcome" means. It is a far more significant word: one implying both "accept" and "welcome into close relationship." And how complete our acceptance is to be! Romans 14:1 uses the same term, and says, "As for the man who is weak in faith, welcome him, but not for disputes over opinions" (RSV). Don't even try to change his views! Welcome him as someone who is *important for himself.*

How do we communicate to a person that he is accepted and welcomed into fellowship? Several ways. (1) We listen to him. In listening we show him that his feelings, experiences, and ideas are important to us: *he* is important. (2) We share with him. We open our lives to him and in sharing invite him to come closer to us as persons — the kind of invitation we give only to people we consider important. (3) We resist the temptation to try to "convert" him. All of us have been in situations where the price of acceptance was *agreeing.* We must resist seeming to want to change a person — even when he's wrong. How can we? By remembering that God is the only one who can work real changes in a person's heart — and our attempts to convince will only communicate to another person that we have put a price on our acceptance, whether we actually have or not! No wonder the Word commands, "Welcome him — but not for disputes over opinions!"

Bear one another's burdens (Gal. 6:1). This too is a unique way to show love and acceptance, in an interaction of expressed concern.

Sometimes we think this verse implies only that we listen to another person's problems and then promise to pray for him or help him. But it means far more; it means that each of us needs to *bare* our burdens as well as bear them!

How does this affirm another person? When we simply listen to *his* needs and show concern, we are actually implying a superior-inferior relationship. We're communicating a sense of being above him . . . and we may be sure that this will only confirm another's low estimate of himself! But when we open ourselves to be *ministered to,* we communicate something else entirely. We show that we value the other person and his ministry. We demonstrate, and thus affirm, that he seems important to us.

Strikingly, when the ministry of bearing burdens is a mutual one, a bearing of *one another's* burdens, then neither person involved comes to see himself as "higher" than another. Instead, each lifts the other up to a higher level *with him!* In bearing one another's burdens, we constantly affirm the value and worth of each other and agree with God that we *are* important. We are worthy of being loved.

Provoke one another (Heb. 10:24). The Revised Standard Version accurately translates the archaic "provoke" into "let us consider how to stir up one another to love and good works."

This is a ministry of affirming one another by showing both trust and expectation. As Christians, we may *expect* God to be working in us. We may expect Him to be working through us. We may expect Him to be changing us. Because Christ is in us, the Bible says, we have hope for all the glorious things that are to come (cf. Col. 1:27 *Phillips*). So we can encourage and stir up each other to act in the faith and confidence that God will act in us!

This is entirely different from struggling to do something we know we can't do because we are so weak and impotent. Or different from trying to prove our value by our accomplishments. This is affirming that in Christ our potential as persons may be realized. *He* is able. Now we can see each other in positive ways. We do not need to live defeated lives or mourn together about our failures. We are so valuable and important to God that He has acted in Christ to free us and to enable us.

How encouraging it is to realize that other Christians think of me now, not as unable, but as enabled! So, by encouraging and expecting each other to act in our newness (yet accepting one another in our humanity should we fail), we testify to each other that the old images of ourselves are wrong. They may be joyfully discarded!

There are others. Ministries that seem on the surface even to be negative — like reproving or rebuking — prove on examination to be affirming. Yet it often is so hard to "speak the truth in love" when we are afraid the truth might hurt or embarrass.

But see what we communicate about the other person when we hold back! We are saying that we don't trust him; that we are afraid he'll take what we say wrongly; or that he is such a weak person he will be unable to bear the truth; or that he is just not important enough for us to run the risk of possible interpersonal discomfort! Yet when something is blocking in a relationship — when there is something that needs to be said and is held back — the barrier is always sensed. And it is always read — rightly — as failure to trust the other person.

Now, this is not to encourage blunt or attacking criticism. This is saying that the truth is to be spoken *in love*. When even a negative truth (a rebuke, or reproof) is spoken in love, it becomes an affirmation of the value of the other person to us and an affirmation of our respect for him.

So also are all the "one another" ways of living together recorded in Scripture. When we learn to live with each other in an affirming, loving fellowship, we release one another from so much that blocks the free working of the Holy Spirit in our hearts and lives.

This, then, is the second element in the life of the group that meets for ministry. We meet to help each other realize who we really are . . . persons of worth and value . . . persons who are the object of God's love . . . persons who can come to accept and love themselves, because we *are* loved.

ACTION IDEAS

Here are some things you may do in a small group to affirm one another. Use them as the members come to know one another and feel a need to bring a low self-image into harmony with God's portrait of the person. (The numbering continues from the ACTION IDEAS on page 37.)

8. *What am I like?*

   Pin a sheet of paper to the back of each group member, and have each write on the others' backs one positive word that best seems to describe the individual.

   When this is done, each person is to take his sheet of paper and, looking at what the others have written, write a brief statement of "what I am like." Each then reads aloud what he has written, giving all the group members opportunity both to add to what has been written and to affirm points that seem particularly significant to them.

9. *How am I important?*

Ask each member of the group to write on paper the names of all the other members. Beside each name should be listed one or more positive things that he contributes to the meaningfulness of your times together. When this has been done, one person is seated in a chair placed slightly in toward the center of the encircling group. Then each person takes a turn speaking directly to the person in the center, saying, "I'm glad you're in our group. . . . " and telling the contribution he listed.

It is important that this affirmation be directed to the individual rather than the group. Don't speak *about* the person in the center . . . speak *to* him.

When done, it may seem appropriate to join hands and pray together or sing a meaningful hymn.

10. *Exploring affirmation*

Pair off the group members and assign one or more of the following verses to each pair:

Romans 12:10	Ephesians 4:2
Romans 15:7 (14:1)	Ephesians 4:32
Romans 15:14	Hebrews 10:24
1 Corinthians 12:25	1 Peter 1:22
Galatians 6:2	1 Peter 5:5

The two are to study the verve and context together and discuss how the situation in Scripture demonstrated affirmation of one another. Then each pair is to agree on at least two other persons in the group who perform this ministry to group members. After twenty minutes, bring all together; have each pair read the verse and speak

57

to the individual they chose, saying, "Jon, we've seen you affirm in this way. When you told Mary last week . . . And when you said . . ."

When all have shared, spend time in prayer simply thanking God for the gifts He has given you in each other.

11. *I can grow*

This activity expresses trust in other members of the group, and at the same time points up weaknesses that need to be dealt with. It involves affirming by reproof!

Give each group member a number of 3x5 cards. On each, the individual is to write the name of a member of the group then on the back complete the following sentence: "I want to see you grow, and trust you to grow, in . . ." Anything that a person sees as an area of need may be mentioned.

" . . . in your freedom to accept yourself."

" . . . in your ability to control your temper."

" . . . in being free of the feeling that someone is attacking you all the time."

" . . . in your willingness to accept others, and not act as though you have to make them see things your way."

More than one 3x5 card may be filled out on a group member for another individual, but each should fill out at least one card for every person. When the cards are completed, each person should be given those filled out about him. Each then may look through the cards and set aside (1) any that puzzle or disturb him and (2) groups of three or more cards that suggest the same area for growth.

Go around the group, with each person reading aloud the cards that puzzle him or show that several in the group see him in a similar light. The person reading should then tell how he feels about what is on the card, and he is free to ask the group, or individuals in the group, *why* they wrote down what they did.

As each individual finishes, the group should take time immediately to pray for him and for the needs explored, both thanking God for the person as he is and thanking God that He is at work in that individual's life, freeing him to grow and to become in Christ.

12. *I am growing*

Have group members spontaneously tell each other the growth they have seen in the time the group has been together and how seeing God at work in specific individuals has ministered to them personally.

13. *Quickie re-entry activities*

These may be used at any time during a group meeting, or at the beginning, to deepen awareness of love for one another.

(a) Name another person, saying to him, "_____, you remind me of [and quote a Bible verse, then tell why]."

(b) Begin or close the meeting by having one person select another, saying, "I've come to love and appreciate you in a special way, because . . . " The person selected takes the hand of the one choosing him and in turn selects another person, forming a chain that finally links all members of the group together.

(c) Each member completes the sentence, "_____ [name another group member] is important to me tonight because . . . "

(d) Each in a single, positive word expresses how he feels to be with the others again.

(e) Each in a single, positive word says something about himself.

59

(f) Join hands and sing together "They'll Know We Are Christians by Our Love."

(g) In sentence prayers thank God for one specific thing about another person in the group.

(h) During the group time, use opportunities to show and tell others they are valued and loved.

SESSION PLAN

The Bible study on pages 119-25 is designed to help the group experience God's and one another's affirmation.

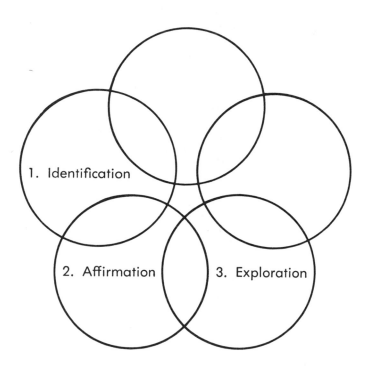

Essential Elements

1. Identification
2. Affirmation
3. Exploration

4

exploration

Some of my driest times spiritually came while I was in seminary, studying the Bible every day. I know it's not supposed to be that way. But it was, for me and for many others.

After all, there's nothing magical about the Bible. A chapter a day doesn't keep the doldrums away. Hours in and out of the classroom getting to know a lot about Scripture won't work like Alice's magic mushroom and transform you into a spiritual giant. Yet the Bible is very important to the health of the group that meets together for ministry.

Discovering God's point of view through Scripture is important for every Christian. *But not as an end in itself.* Getting into the Bible together is important as a means — a means that God uses to bring our life and thoughts and actions into harmony with Him and each other. The Bible is a means He uses to transform us and our experience.

It's with this realization that we need to approach God's Word in our small groups. The Bible is not just for learning, but for living.

We desperately need Scripture to guide us in our living.

The reason for this is simple. Reality is so often hidden from us. The appearances of things around us deceive. Illusions masquerade and blind our senses so that what we perceive as true, as real, as helpful, is often utterly false.

For instance, a "crusading psychologist," Dr. Robert L. Wolk, recently published a book on *The Right to Lie.** His thesis is that if children are taught to tell lies, when they do lie they'll avoid "ego-damaging guilt"; thus, in various situations lying is the best way possible to show love. If youngsters learn to use lies considerately and appropriately, they will be better able to "cope with the demands of reality."

But do we know reality? Will a lie really preserve us from harm or show love for others? Is life really like this — some thing we may manipulate with lies? Or is the idea that lies can make a positive contribution to the happiness of others merely an illusion — a shadow cast by a sin-warped perception of life? How do we know what life is *really* like?

The Bible hints that one of the links in the chain binding us to our humanity is the fact that we are blind to reality. We're blind, but we think we see. In Ephesians, Paul calls this distorted idea of life "this world's ideas of living" (2:2 *Phillips*). John speaks bluntly of walking in light and darkness. He warns that if we deny revealed reality, "we live

---

* Robert L. Wolk and Arthur Henley, *The Right to Lie: A Psychological Guide to the Uses of Deceit in Everyday Life* (New York: Peter H. Wyden, 1970).

in a world of illusion and truth becomes a stranger to us" (1 John 1:8 *Phillips*).

Throughout the Bible, "truth" and "reality" display an intimate connection. "Truth" in Old and New Testaments, in the original languages, implies the concept of "in full harmony with reality," of "an accurate portrait of the way things really are." We see this connection clearly in the 1 John passage (vv. 5-10).

Here God is presented as Light, with no shadow of darkness existing in Him. To enjoy fellowship with Him, the believer cannot go on "living in darkness." To claim fellowship with such a God while we live in darkness is both "telling and living a lie" (v. 6 *Phillips*).

But what is "darkness"? Is it sin? No, it's not! Even in fellowship, John says, we must still rely on the blood of Christ to keep on cleansing us from all sin. John's talk of light and dark is not of sin, *but of reality!* "If we refuse to admit that we are sinners," he says (v. 8), we live in that world of illusion and lose contact with truth. We must come to see ourselves as we are and honestly face our helplessness and inadequacy. Failing to face the fact of sin keeps us struggling to perform, "but if we freely admit that we have sinned," the Word continues, "we find God utterly reliable and straightforward — he forgives our sins and makes us thoroughly clean from all that is evil. For if we take up the attitude 'we have not sinned,' we flatly deny God's diagnosis of our condition and cut ourselves off from what he has to say to us" (1 John 1:8-10 *Phillips*).

"Darkness," then, speaks of *denial of God's diagnosis* and *failure to live in harmony with it!* "Light," on the other hand, speaks of reality as it is known

65

and revealed by God. So, to know reality as God knows it, to respond to life guided by His perceptions of what is real, is walking in the light.

This is what Bible study is all about! We study the Bible to distinguish reality from illusion — and we stake our lives on the trustworthiness of God's revelation by determining to *live* by the Word.

A basic choice

This is an utterly basic choice the Christian has to make and stand by.

And it's so reasonable. God alone has a vantage point from which to see reality. He alone is able to diagnose, to share an accurate perception of reality with us. He alone knows Truth.

But in the Scripture He has revealed it.

Sometimes people make a distinction between Scripture as a "relational" book and a book of "objective" or "propositional" truth. The two ideas, though, are not to be seen in *contrast,* but in their relationship to each other. God's Word *is* relational truth: every expression of the Word is to be read through Christ, and every expression shows us how to live in harmonious relationship with God or ourselves or others or our universe. But it is because God's Word is true — reality communicated in and as true information — that the relationships we may experience through the Word are possible. Unless we want to lose ourselves in darkness, we must accept the diagnosis of God's Word, accept the reality revealed, and pattern our lives fully on His truth.

So we have to choose.

And the choice we must make — and help each

other hold firmly to as we meet for ministry — is to *do* the Word of God.

A burden?

There's something both safe and harmless in a Bible that we meet to debate over. If the Bible is just information, merely ideas to hold detached discussions about, then we need feel no compulsion to change or to act. But when we see Scripture as Truth and Light, something to illuminate life and show us how to live it, we develop a deep sense of burden.

Life is difficult enough as it is. If there is *more* we are supposed to do and to be, how may we bear it?

But when we understand the full implications of what it means to say, "The Bible reveals reality," even that burden is removed! We no longer have to hear the words of Scripture as a demand. We may hear them as *an invitation to experience reality.*

Some time ago I read a book on prayer that terrorized me. It took a number of familiar verses and constructed a set of "seven conditions" for getting answers. If these conditions were fulfilled, the author said, prayer would be answered. Otherwise we had little hope.

The idea disturbed me, but as verse was piled on verse I became convinced. The Bible *did* teach "conditions" for answered prayer! I could see no way out.

— "When you pray in faith, believing, you shall receive."

— "When you ask anything in God's will."

67

And my heart sank. I knew my prayers more often expressed hesitation than faith. I knew that often I was uncertain about His will. And I felt trapped, cut off from God by obstacles I couldn't overcome.

Then I learned to see the Word of God as reality — and everything changed. The "conditions" took on new form, and I learned something of the differences between "if" and "then."

What differences? Let's see, by looking at two situations. (1) A mother is watching TV. Her son comes in the door, and, without taking her eyes off the set, she warns him: "If you walk in front of me and block my view, I'll club you!" A conditional statement has been made. (2) Another mother is cooking dinner when her son comes in. She sees him look inquiringly toward the stove, and warns, "If you touch that pot, you'll get burned." Again, a conditional statement has been made — but what a difference!

The first statement we must regard as a selfish demand, a coercive attempt to force the child to the mother's will. The second we regard as love. There's no coercion here, and it is clearly the child's good the mother has in view. The harm arises from the natural consequences of disregarding the reality of the hotness of the pot — a reality the child was made aware of by the mother's statement. The form of both mothers' statements is the same — conditional — *but the motive and tone of voice and what is being communicated make them entirely different!*

It's the same with the Bible. Is God shouting conditions and demands, like the first mother, and warning us of dire consequences if we dare displease Him? Or is our God like the second mother

68

— enlightening, loving, opening up the possibility of new ways to live by showing us the reality of what will harm us and what will help? We have no doubts. God *loves* us. His every word is spoken in the honest tones of love.

How then am I to understand the "conditions" associated with prayer? As the promise of a reality that in Christ I may pray in faith, believing. To do so is a reality that I may experience — and in experiencing, *know* that my prayer is being answered. To know His will is a possibility, a thing that is really possible, and this too I may experience. It is just this — to experience more reality in prayer than I have — to which these verses invite me.

God is not shouting His demands at me.

God is inviting me closer, showing me what blessings He has in store!

But what of our humanness?

To realize that the Bible is God's portrait of reality and His invitation to experience reality helps me throw off the guilt and shame that grip a person when he feels, "I ought . . . " God's Word does not pile burdens on us; it opens doors!

At this point I'm again struck by my humanness. I catch a fresh awareness of my inability even to accept His invitation. *The Bible may describe reality — but where do I go for power to experience it!*

Here a third dimension of Bible study comes in, one that completes and vitalizes the first two. Remember, we've seen so far that

— the Bible is for our living (not just learning).

— the Bible reveals a reality we are to experience.

69

But whenever we *try* to experience what Scripture speaks of, we discover again how human and weak we are. *How* do I approach Scripture to find it becoming true in me?

The answer God gives us is very simple.

We approach the Bible in faith.

With confidence.

Too often we approach living by Scriptures by making an "honest effort," or "trying." This is how many believers describe their Christian lives. But the very words reveal a tragic misconception — a retreat in relationship with God from a grace to a performance (or works) basis.

It's hard to grasp, but perhaps we can see that even to speak of faith as "trying" turns attention to ourselves. It assumes, to some extent at least, that *we,* not Christ, are responsible for our lives. When we turn back to ourselves for resources to experience God's reality, we find ourselves trapped in the impotence of our humanity.

The same Bible that reveals reality teaches us to cast off *all* thought of performance and fixes our attention on Christ. Peter walked safely on the waves as long as his gaze was fixed on the Lord. But he sank when that gaze was distracted. We too are invited by the Word to keep our eyes on Christ; we are told that God's plan is to *impart* righteousness, not demand it. And this, the Bible says, is a process begun and continued by faith. So, the Scripture reminds, "the righteous shall live by faith" (Rom. 1:17 *Phillips*).

Some time ago my children had a peculiar game. It consisted of some clear plastic over a cardboard square, enclosing metallic dust, and a magnet. For hours the children would sit and shape and reshape that dust with the magnet. They formed faces, little men, animals, all sorts of things. The dust responded to the magnet's pull.

Faith operates this way. It would be foolish to talk of the dust moving by "its magnetic power." The power rests in the magnet; the dust merely responds. It would be just as foolish to speak of "faith" as though it were some power in us. We respond. The power to change is God's.

So "living by faith" takes on a peculiar character. *We respond to God's Word as to One who is utterly faithful.*

This is the "new spiritual principle of life 'in' Christ Jesus [that] lifts me out of the old vicious circle of sin and death" (Rom. 8:1 *Phillips*). *Christ lives in me.* His power frees. Turning away from every thought of strength or trying, we are free to respond to the promptings of the Spirit through His Word.

"Faith" faces the reality of who we are — the reality of humanity and our weakness. But faith responds to *do* the Word of God, expecting nothing from ourselves! Faith responds to *do* in the amazing conviction that *in the doing* Christ's own power and Christ's own life will actually control and enable us!

We can step out and obey the Word of God because Christ *is* in us. He brings us hope for glorious things to come.

The place of the Word

When a group meets for ministry, the Scripture must play a central role in the experience. We may summarize the particular functions of the Bible in the group meeting this way.

(1) The Bible is explored for light and truth.

We know that God's revelation gives us an accurate picture of every reality we need to understand. We come to see God as He is; we come to understand ourslves; we discover how we may live to please God and experience His joy and love.

Some groups approach the Bible from the point of view of personal problems. In their sharing they discover something that troubles them, and they want answers. Recently a small group my wife and I were in saw several members uncertain about prayer. During the next weeks we each studied the Bible and then brought what we'd learned to the group meeting for discussion. In those weeks each person's nagging uncertainties were settled, and we found a fresh confidence in God as real questions were answered by Him.

Other groups begin with a common passage of Scripture and study it to determine just what God is showing us about reality. Either approach is suitable for a small group. But unless the Bible does have a central role in the groups' experience, the group will not realize its full potential. We *are* subject to illusion. We desperately need to check our every thought and perception against the portrait of reality God has lovingly given in the Scriptures.

(2) The Bible is for living, not simply for learning. God's objective revelation of truth is always to be explored in view of its impact on human experience.

Here a group study makes a unique contribution. When each person shares "Here's how I see this truth affecting my life," our vision expands. The Holy Spirit works through each of us to illumine and make clear the *meaning to me* of what God has said to us all.

When group members have learned to relate openly and honestly with one another, experiencing both the identification and affirmation aspects of group life, they are freed to share (and to see) what the Bible means to them.

It is vital that whenever the Bible is studied, we move together from "what is revealed" to state clearly "what this means to me."

(3) The Word is to be experienced. This last element simply means that we are to *do* what we've seen in Scripture. We are to obey, to "continue in" Christ's words, to "keep My words."

To act.

Here, too, we need to share. We may share both what we have done in obedience to the Word and what we feel God wants us to do this coming week.

This kind of sharing is important. In it we may remind each other to step out in faith: we can rely on God to make the act of obedience possible in us. We may pray for each other, a vital ministry in view of the fact that it is Jesus' supernatural power at work in us — and that our God answers prayer.

This sharing is particularly important as encouragement. When, week after week, we see God actually working out His life in others who have responded in faith to the Word, we find our own trust in God increasing. When we see God working in others, we sense in new ways the presence and the power of God in us. Then we're moved to praise and to trust Him even more.

ACTION IDEAS

Here are some ways you may study the Bible — first, individually in preparation for group meetings

73

and, second, when you are gathered during the group time. (The numbering continues from the ACTION IDEAS on page 59.)

Studying the Bible in preparation.

14. *Outline the portion or passage you are studying*

    There are a number of ways to outline, but one of the simplest and best is to write a single sentence that seems to sum up a paragraph or short segment of the section you are studying. For example, here is an outline, in sentence form, of Habakkuk 2.

    God seems to be telling Habakkuk (2:1-20) that the sinner never really gets away with anything. *Any* sinner. Why?

    a. The arrogant never has enough (2:1-6) — he can't find satisfaction.

    b. Others are going to pay him back (2:7, 8) — his actions give them scores to settle!

    c. He can never be really secure — (2:9-11) his way of life keeps him in danger.

    d. Only good is going to last — sin (2:12-14) and its works will be destroyed in the end.

    e. (Don't understand this one.) (2:15-17)

    f. Trusting false gods is useless — (2:18, 19) only God is alive and able to act.

    See what a quick and striking "picture of reality" this approach can give!

15. *React*

    As you read a passage, argue against it! Jot down all the objections to the picture of reality it seems to be giving. Think really hard to get good objections — and then try to answer each

74

one. In the process, you'll gain a surprisingly sharp understanding of what is being said!

For instance, try this technique with Ephesians 5:21-33 if you are in a group of couples.

16. *Paraphrase*

Often the Bible uses familiar phrases and words that may not be used in the context in the way we think of them. When this happens, we're forced to find out what a word or phrase does mean, in context, if we are to understand the passage and glimpse the reality it reveals.

One of the best ways of doing this is to paraphrase: to put in our own words (*not* using words in the text, but finding synonyms) the thoughts and sentences of the passage.

For instance, James 2:14-26 uses "faith" and "justified" in ways we have to dig into to understand. Why not try paraphrasing this passage?

17. *Identification*

One of the most helpful ways of studying the Bible is to identify with a person being talked about or talked to. How does he feel? When have I felt this way? How did he react in the situation? Have I been in similar situations? How did I react? What did God say to this person? What would He be likely to say to me today — the same thing? something different? Why?

Since the Bible is for living, it is helpful in seeking its picture of reality to enter into the lives of the people whose experiences are recorded for our example!

For example, read Psalm 74 and see if you have lived through the experiences the psalmist relates.

18. *Word studies*

Often selecting key words and studying them

give us insights into a passage. Various tools might be used for such a study, including concordances and lexicons. One helpful approach is to select key words and then try to find the synonym that most accurately restates the thought of the passage.

For example, Ephesians 1:3-14 contains a number of verbs that express God's involvement in our salvation. Make a list of these words, then look for the best synonym for each.

19. *Tone of voice*

Read aloud a passage of Scripture, trying at first to read in an angry, demanding tone — like the one a person might expect from the first mother (page 68). Then ask another person to read, trying to reflect a tone of voice appropriate to the second mother (page 68). Talk together about the differences the tone of voice makes in how group members "hear" the passage.

Talk, too, about how the members have been hearing the Bible and any impact this may have made on their attitude about the Scripture.

A passage you might want to use is Colossians 3:1-10.

20. *Identify and relate*

Select an incident for group study. Spend eight to ten minutes individually thinking about the person(s) the incident involves. Try to understand how each must have felt, and why he did so.

Then share your understanding of the person(s) and ideas about him (them). When this has been done, individually decide "In what way or ways am I like Him? How does what God taught him apply to me now?" Share this with the group and explore together the needs revealed.

(For a developed example of this kind of study, see the plan for group study, page 112-17.)

Two passages you might enjoy taking this approach with are Mark 1:40-45, and Matthew 16:21-23.

21. *Sharing reality*

Give each group member a 3x5 card on which to write a verse conveying a command or exhortation which usually makes him feel discouraged, inadequate, or guilty because of failure to measure up.

Mix the cards randomly and distribute them so that each group member has someone else's card.

Then give each person 15 minutes to *restate* the verse so its nature as reality rather than demand may be seen. Each should also write a brief description of ways in which an experience of that reality might be known.

For instance, a person might write down a verse on witnessing, reflecting his fear to speak to another about Christ. After restating the verse to emphasize it as a statement about the possibility of experiencing reality, another person may give a description like the following: "When you experience this, you don't feel afraid to witness — in fact you don't really even think about it much. Instead, it simply begins to seem natural to talk about Jesus when opportunities come. And you don't feel that you've got to convert the other person; instead, you just kind of relax and are willing to let God do that. So you don't have to press, or feel pressure."

When all have done this, the group reconvenes. One person first reads the verse, his restatement of it, and the descriptive paragraph he wrote. The others (1) comment on his interpretation, suggesting additions or raising questions and (2) share times when they have actually experienced the reality this verse speaks of. This second thing is the more important.

For greater depth. The person who wrote the verse on the card in the first place shares with the group why this one has bothered him, and he invites the prayers of the others as he asks God to help him learn the reality of this particular truth in his life during the coming week.

22. *Research*

For greater depth you may want to study together sections of the author's book, *Creative Bible Study* (Grand Rapids: Zondervan, 1971). To focus on the attitude with which we approach Scripture (of confident expectation and awareness of God's inviting tone), see chapters 2 through 9. To develop specific skills in studying the Bible, to move from needs to find God's solution in Scripture, and to begin with Scripture and move to application to life, see chapters 10 through 16. Each chapter concludes with suggestions for group activities which will help readers experience the concepts explored.

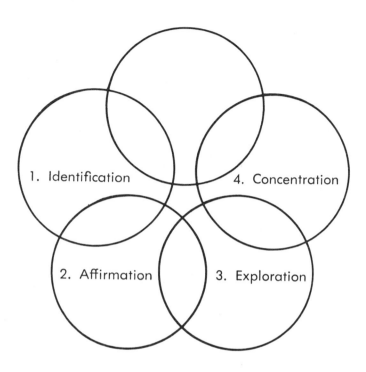

Essential Elements

1. Identification
2. Affirmation
3. Exploration
4. Concentration

5

concentration

It happened again Sunday. We started our time together looking at the key verse — "all things were created by him, and for him [Jesus]" (Col. 1:16) — and then went around the class asking each person to complete the sentence, "I was made for Jesus to . . ." The adults came up with some exciting things. I was made for Jesus, different members suggested,

to trust Him	to be a good steward
to worship Him	to do His work
to be a good father	to be like Him
to relax in Him and	to enjoy life
be a channel	to thank Him

etc.

It's deeply moving to realize afresh that "Christ Himself is the Creator who made everything in heaven and earth, the things we can see and the things we can't" (v. 16 *Living Bible*) and that you and I are among all that was made by Him and for Him! Yet, as we explored together, Dave (a newcomer to our class) commented, as he contributed "to witness," that "I believe that's my obligation.

81

I'd like to think of it as a privilege, but right now I feel it is an obligation."

I was made by Jesus and for Jesus. Must the realization of who we are and who God is bring with it a feeling of burden and obligation?

Certainly it has had this impact. In Nehemiah's day the Jewish people were returning from exile in Babylon. Called to Jerusalem, there they heard for the first time the Word of God read and taught clearly (Neh. 8:7, 8). The Bible says "all the people wept, when they heard the words of the law" (v. 9). They were suddenly overwhelmed in realizing all they were not and all they had not done. The Word came to them. They heard it as obligation. And they were crushed.

But the leaders responded, "This day is holy to the LORD your God; do not mourn or weep. . . . Go your way, eat the fat and drink sweet wine and send portions to him for whom nothing is prepared; for this day is holy to our Lord; and do not be grieved, for the joy of the LORD is your strength" (vv. 9, 10 RSV). Don't hear the Law only as a revelation of your weakness. This day — this day of looking into the Word — is set aside to the Lord. See Him and realize that the joy of the Lord is your strength.

What a difference in the two approaches to Scripture.

The one fastens on and looks at self as our human limitations are reflected against His standards. The other looks beyond self to see the Lord and finds in Him rejoicing and strength.

Strength

We saw in an earlier chapter that sharing in a small group is to take place on a dual level: the level of our humanity and the level of our experience with Jesus. The first level we called a *static* level because, while we find some initial relief in sharing our needs and problems and in being accepted as we are, there is no power in this kind of relationship. This fact is borne out by behavioral science research, which shows that groups begin characteristically with high levels of enthusiasm but over a period of time fail to meet expectations. Disappointment sets in.

But for the group meeting for ministry, there is a *dynamic* level of relationship that is open. On this dynamic level, significant changes *do* take place; growth and transformation occur. And the critical factor in living together on this level? *To share our experience of Jesus and to concentrate on helping each other see just who He is for us.*

We can help each other look away from ourselves and the burden of obligation. We can help each other look to Jesus and find strength through joy in Him.

That is what the title of this chapter suggests. We are to accept and be ourselves with each other. We are to affirm and love each other. We are to study the Word together. But in it all we are to concentrate on Jesus. We are to seek to grasp more and more of who He is. Paul's prayer for the Ephesians seems to sum up what we need in our ministry groups:

> . . . the eyes of your hearts enlightened, that you may know what is the hope to which he has called you, what are the riches of his glorious inheritance in the saints,
>
> and what is the immeasurable greatness of his power in us who believe,

according to the working of his great might which he accomplished in Christ when he raised him from the dead and made him sit at his right hand in the heavenly places (Eph. 1:18-20 RSV).

We are an inheritance for Him, and He glories in us. His power in us is immeasurable, and we are to glory in Him. When we realize who Jesus is, we are free to joy in Him, and then we find the strength to grow and change.

It helps, then, to bring into focus just who Jesus is for us and to remind each other, as we read the Word and share, that it is *this Jesus,* not ourselves, not even God's standards, on whom we concentrate.

Who is Jesus for us?

Most members in a group meeting for ministry will know Jesus as Savior. But Christ's work is not fully summed up in the redemption and forgiveness that come to us with our first faith in Him. That's the beginning, yes. But He goes beyond. He totally involves Himself in our whole life and experience. He is the victor . . . victor over Satan, over sin, and even over the poverty and weakness of His adopted brothers.

We may see Jesus in several of these "victor" roles in Scripture.

Jesus, overcomer. The miracles of Jesus are often pointed to as authenticating His claim to Deity. They do this. But they do far more.

The Jews who clustered around Jesus were seeking a Messiah — someone who would claim royal power and overthrow the Roman oppressors, which in that day controlled Palestine as well as most of the western world. Yet, as Jesus continued to minister and teach, He seemed to take no steps to-

84

ward assuming political power. Many were puzzled. Even His cousin, John the Baptist, who had first announced Him as Messiah, was uncertain. John had been jailed by Herod. Perhaps John's doubt was only the natural depression of an active man, a man with a sense of mission, cut off from activity. But doubt he did. At last he sent followers to ask Jesus if He were the One who was to come or if they should look for another. The Bible tells us what the Lord sent John's followers to report: "Go and tell John what you hear and see: the blind receive their sight and the lame walk, lepers are cleansed, and the deaf hear, and the dead are raised up, and the poor have the good news preached to them" (Matt. 11:4, 5 RSV).

What a catalog of miracles! But, more significantly, *what* miracles! Every one of the miracles Jesus mentioned is a miracle that meets the desperate needs of men and women.

If Jesus were concerned only with authenticating His claim to be Messiah, what startling things He might have done! Elijah and Elisha made fire fall from heaven — Jesus could have. Moses struck the waters, and they opened — Jesus could have. Joshua saw the sun stand still — Jesus could have commanded, and it would have blinked out! But Jesus' miracles were those that meet the needs of people. Jesus' miracles overcame human infirmities.

See what is revealed? First, that even when glorifying Himself, God is deeply concerned with individuals. Second, that Jesus' limitless power is focused on one thing — overcoming the infirmities of men.

And this is the Jesus we know today! This overcomer, who focused His power to enable the unable, is our God. He is ready to do exactly this in our lives today!

Suzie and her husband are new Christians. Immediately after his conversion John began to share Christ with the men on the job. It didn't affect his work; John's the conscientious type — overly conscientious, Suzie sometimes thinks. But John's witnessing really upset his supervisor. Finally the supervisor, by lying, got John fired. The more John thought about it, the more hurt and angry he became. Bitterness grew . . . until suddenly John realized what was happening to his attitude. He couldn't change it or root out the hurt, so he turned it over to Jesus. And God brought him a great peace and calm.

As John shared this in church with us, he began by thanking God for the new job He had provided in answer to our prayers. But it was clear that what meant most to him was the joy of seeing God work in his personality. To see Christ give him the freedom to forgive!

Jesus is overcomer today. What is your infirmity? Your weakness? your need? Look to Jesus, and see Him focusing all the power of God to meet that need and to free you to glorify Him.

Jesus, Lord. When we see Jesus, we have to be gripped by the consciousness that He is Lord. Paul goes on in the Ephesians passage quoted earlier to point out that the resurrected Jesus is seated at the Father's right hand,

> far above all rule and authority and power and dominion, and above every name that is named, not only in this age but also in that which is to come; and he has put all things under his feet and has made him the head over all things for the

church, which is his body, the fulness of him who fills all in all (Eph. 1:21-23 RSV).

Jesus' lordship has a multiple impact for us. First, because Jesus is Lord we are free to accept all that God brings into our lives with joy and in peace. Jesus is "far above" *all* rule and authority. Jesus is in charge. Knowing His love for us, we may rest in the confidence that all He permits is an active gift of love for us.

Sometimes this is hard to believe. Brad, a teen in our church. was lying near death from cancer. His mom and dad sat with him, suffering their own unique pain. Yet in the experience, seeing Jesus as Lord brought peace. Brad expressed his readiness to be with the Lord. And one night, as his mother — ached with the pain of seeing her son suffer — felt she could stand it no more, she turned to the Lord and gave Brad freely back to Him. Brad was to be fully His, not hers. And then peace came.

Jesus is Lord. His rule means for us His protective care and guidance. But even when His choice involves us in some pain or suffering, we may know that He is Lord and find peace in remembering that He is also Love.

Second, Jesus' lordship means that He is our Head. As our Head, Jesus directs our lives and leads us. How good to know we're not left to ourselves and our own understanding as we struggle to make our choices. We may *know* what is best: through principles He shares in His Word, then, through the guiding ministry of the Holy Spirit as He leads each individual into the distinctive path of life God has planned for him.

Jesus is Lord.

Seeing Him as Lord, we give Him full control, and we let Him be Lord to us.

Jesus, indweller. A third theme we need to grasp to realize who Jesus is for us is expressed in the idea of "indwelling." Jesus is not an absentee God. He is not even merely a model, someone whom we look away to, to see what our life ought to be like. It is true that He is our example. "Follow Me," Jesus said, and He implied both an imitation and a commitment to His lordship.

But Jesus makes it possible for us to follow Him by being present with us! Luke opens the Book of Acts with a reminder that he has previously written a gospel to share "all that Jesus began to do and teach" (1:1 RSV). Now Luke is to continue, reporting in Acts all that Jesus keeps on doing and teaching — in the persons of believers! Jesus has not left us. Jesus is here, now, *doing* in and through us.

Because Jesus lives in us, we may live in Him.

Each of these portraits of Jesus helps us to concentrate on Him when we explore Scripture and our lives. When we understand who Jesus is for us, then we can begin to experience His Word with joy, and do that word with strength. We can't do it ourselves. But Jesus can — and will.

> Jesus is the overcomer. He will overcome our weaknesses and free us from the infirmities that keep us from growth and change.
>
> Jesus is Lord. He is in control of the universe and every circumstance that confronts us. He is eager to guide and to direct us as we give Him control over our lives.
>
> Jesus is within. We may be like Him, for He is with us to express His love and concern for people through us.

88

If we know Jesus in these ways — as overcomer, Lord, and indweller — our whole life changes. We suddenly discover that life cannot be summed up in our limitations. We *can* live beyond ourselves.

The touch of Jesus

Many Christians find it hard to see Jesus as we've just viewed Him. They're eager to sense the touch of Jesus in their lives but have settled down to live in quiet desperation, convinced against their will that there is reality for them only beyond the grave and in the resurrection.

But Jesus dealt with such concerns thoroughly in His Upper Room discourse, particularly in answer to a question from one of His disciples: "Lord, how is it that you will manifest yourself to us, and not to the world?" (John 14:22 RSV). It was a good question, a vital one: Jesus, how do You make Yourself plainly and clearly visible to Your own people — without being seen by men of the world? Jesus' answer was simple, yet pointed: "If a man loves me, he will keep my word, and my Father will love him, and we will come to him and make our home with him" (v. 23).

Love produces obedience.

And in obedience the reality of God's presence is made plain.

It shouldn't be hard to understand this. Sometimes we try to obey out of a sense of duty. Then obedience is a grudging struggle, an attempt to do what we feel God demands of us. But this is always doomed to failure. We're not able to do all we should. When we approach Scripture and live with this attitude, we experience only the reality of our own inadequacy. No matter how hard we try, we fail (cf. Rom. 7:15).

But sometimes we're moved by love to obey. And what a different focus! Love doesn't think of itself; love fixes its eyes on the loved one. When this happens, we're aware of Jesus, and we discover in amazement that we have done what we could never do before! In forgetting ourselves and thinking of Jesus, we have moved from the *static* to the *dynamic* in life, and we actually experience the reality of Jesus' adequacy.

There are two realities that we may experience.

(1) The reality of our inadequacy.
(2) The reality of Jesus' adequacy.

When we concentrate on Jesus and love for Him, Jesus fulfills His promise that His disciples will "keep my words." In the actual doing of the word, which requires this divine enabling, we experience God's power. *And it is in this experience of God's power that we plainly see Jesus!*

Throughout the significant Upper Room chapters (John 13 - 17), this thought is emphasized and re-emphasized. "Abide in me," Jesus encourages. "Live close to Me." How? "If you keep my commandments, you will abide in my love, just as I have kept my Father's commandments and abide in His love" (John 15:10 RSV). Staying close to Jesus involves loving Him, love-motivated obedience, and the actual experience of Jesus' enabling us to live beyond ourselves.

When this is your experience and mine, we have no more questions about the reality of Jesus. We have touched Him, and He has touched our lives. We have felt His presence. We *know.*

So, meeting for ministry is even more clearly

seen. We meet to study the Bible — but not to find rules to keep. Not to find new doctrines or to defend our old ones. Not because knowing more about the Bible will make us better or "more spiritual." We study the Bible to see Jesus as enabler, as Lord, as present with us.

When we see Him as enabler, we realize that, whatever the Word says, we need not feel crushed or under obligation. We may hear that word with joy and find strength in Him to obey.

When we see Him as Lord, we realize that whatever the Word says to us, we are to commit ourselves to it.

When we see Him as present with us, we realize He has not left us to struggle alone. He Himself takes up every burden and bears it for us. When we see Him as *this kind of God,* we are moved to love Him, and through love we are moved to obey.

And so we come full circle.

In obedience, we feel His touch. We know His working in our lives, and come to love Him even more.

This is our ministry to each other in the small group. To help each other see Jesus and all He is for us. And to help each other love and trust Him even more.

ACTION IDEAS

Here are several things your group might do to help each other focus on who Jesus is and what He is doing in each life. Seeing Jesus at work, enabling and empowering, is a vital stimulus to deepening our own faith and confidence in Him. (The numbering is continued from the ACTION IDEAS on page 78.)

23. *Portraits of Jesus*
    Have various members of your group share how
    they see Jesus, and tie in their portraits either to
    Scripture or to their personal experiences of His
    love. There are many variations to this approach.
    Your group may select a gospel incident and
    examine how the disciples might have seen Jesus.
    Or the crowd. Or Satan (a very disgruntled on-
    looker!).

24. *Memorization*
    A verse like Colossians 1:16 ("all created by
    Him and for Him") may be assigned for memo-
    rization and meditation. When the group assem-
    bles, do what the class described in the chapter
    did. Each completed the statement "I was made
    for Jesus to . . . " and shared one way in which
    they realized they were made for Him and could
    glorify Him.

25. *Focused Bible study*
    Select a passage of Scripture and focus on what
    it reveals about the Lord and His relationship to
    you. For instance, here is part of a study guide
    to Ephesians used in a small group in Phoenix,
    Arizona.

    > List the verbs in Ephesians 1:3-14 that tell
    > what God has done in providing salvation,
    > and beside each give a synonym which seems
    > to you to best restate the idea.

Record now which of these activities best communicates to you a sense of God's love for you. Why?

26. *Jesus in me this week*

How have we seen Jesus in our lives this week? This is a basic question, and ought to provide a central element in sharing each time a group meets. Rehearsing what the Lord has done in us and for us is the heart of building awareness of Jesus and who He is for us.

27. *Giving gifts*

As needs are expressed or shared, a group may stop and have each member give, in Jesus' name, a particular gift to the person who has expressed concern. The goal is for each to try to see the person sharing as Jesus sees him, and then to communicate what the Lord is able to do in his life.

For instance, one group member might share frustration in working with another person in her office and the tears that come at home after another day of tension and bickering. The other group members might then begin to give gifts — the kind of gifts Jesus is eager and willing and able to give.

— "Ruth, in Jesus' name, I want to give you a peaceful spirit, to quiet the upset you feel."

— "Ruth, in Jesus' name, I want to give you a forgiving spirit, to wash out some of the bitterness that must be building up."

— "Ruth, in Jesus' name, I want to give you a loving spirit, to overcome the negativism there and reach out to help the other person, who must be hurting too."

Giving gifts may be done at any time in a group meeting, or it may be a part of the group's life, planned for every third or fourth session as a regular closing feature.

28. *Expressed commitment*

Response to God's Word as loving obedience is central in experiencing the presence of Christ. A group may help individuals not only see varous ways discovered truths can be applied to life, but also motivate and encourage follow-through.

After study of a passage, each individual may select and share one way the Holy Spirit is leading him to act on the Word that week. Closing prayer time can focus on prayer for strength to follow through on commitments individuals in the group have expressed.

29. *Support partners*

Pair off members of the group (*not* by husband and wife) and have each person responsible to call his partner at least once during the week, to share how expressed commitments are being experienced, or problems and needs. Each should pray daily and specifically for his partner and remind one another of Christ's presence and sufficiency.

SESSION PLAN

The Bible study on pages 133-37 is designed to help the group focus on Jesus.

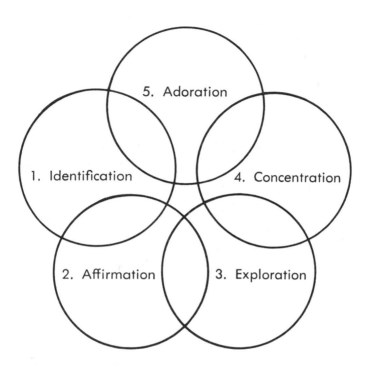

Essential Elements

1. Identification
2. Affirmation
3. Exploration
4. Concentration
5. Adoration

6

adoration

We know little of worship these days. So often our church services, after a few hymns, concentrate on the proclamation of the Word and exhortation — but then fall short of leading us on to worship God.

I think probably I first experienced worship in seminary. Not in the classes or in our daily chapels, but in a motel near campus where I worked at night. There I found much time to study the Bible. I started working through my New Testament, using the language tools I was gaining in my daytime studies, and I began to discover in fresh and new ways what God was communicating to me. It was really unexpected. But after I had dug into the Word for an hour or two, without any planning or effort, I would find myself praying and simply thanking God for who He is and for letting me see Him just a little more clearly.

I have a similar experience in the church our family attends. There, after a message from Scripture I hear the church family share their week. They share prayer requests, report answers to prayer, expose honestly and clearly God's working in people's lives. And there, too, as in Bible study,

I begin to see the Lord in a fresher, clearer way. Worship and praise spring up in my heart.

Affirming God

There is reason to believe that worship is our first and perhaps dearest response to the Lord. The great evidence of the corruption sin brings, as Paul mentions in Romans 1, is that, when men knew what could be known about God in creation, "they did not honor him as God or give thanks to him" (v. 21 RSV). Sensing who God is, we are always to express to Him our praise and thanks and to tell Him how good and wonderful He is to us.

Such worship is an essential part of the life of a group meeting for ministry simply because it is an essential part of every person's relationship with the Lord. The ministry group meets to deepen relationships — not simply the horizontal relationships between members of the Body of Christ, but the vertical relationship between each participant and the Lord. When we have a deeper sense of who He is, we are free to develop a deeper relationship with each other. For the basis of interpersonal unity is the fact that we are one *in* Christ. Jesus Himself, then, must always be the focus of our shared life. As we come to know Him better, we *respond to Him* and help each other respond to Him — in obedience, yes, but first in worship.

A response. I have suggested something I think is very important. Worship must be viewed as a response to God. Worship isn't something we can program; it isn't something we can "turn on" with stately music or by the awesomeness of some great cathedral. Worship is a response to God Himself, and it comes when the believer meets Him afresh — when God reveals Himself to us. So worship may come at any time during experience of a group when God's presence is sensed . . . but it probably cannot be "programmed."

The Word. One of the channels through which God reveals Himself — the primary one — is the Scriptures. Thus, worship in the group normally will follow a sharing in the Word — a time when God's greatness and goodness has been seen again. (How peculiar that most of our church services seem designed to expect people to worship *before* God has revealed Himself afresh in the preached word!)

Our lives. Another primary channel through which God reveals Himself is our lives. We saw in the preceding chapter that Jesus makes Himself plainly known to the one who loves Him when that person, moved by love, obeys. How rich an experience when we gather weekly to hear how each of us has experienced a touch of Jesus' hand during our week! And how exciting it is to see Him *alive* through His work in the life of a brother or sister whom we're coming to love.

While hymns and stately buildings or nature itself may turn some people's hearts to God and stimulate worship, His primary means of revelation remain the Word and the lives of believers. And these two sources of His self-revelation are exactly those on which the small group builds.

When we meet for ministry, then, and when we see Him, we need to be free to stop, to speak directly to Him, and give Him our praise and worship for who He is.

ACTION IDEAS

There are a number of spontaneous and planned ways in which a group may join in adoration of the Lord. Here are a few of them, which may be initiated by any group member at an appropriate time, or which when followed through can give a group a variety of options for worship. (The numbering continues from the ACTION IDEAS on page 94.)

30. *Songs*

    Build a repertoire of simple, short worship songs and hymns. For several weeks, teach a new song as the meeting opens. Then, with the music held in common, any member of the group can start a known song when moved to praise. (Do *not* use song sheets in your meetings; they tend to limit spontaneity.)

31. *Pattern prayer on Psalms*

    Select an appropriate praise psalm (cf. Pss. 66, 93, 96, 98, 100, 105, 111, and others) to use in one of the following ways:

    — Pray a verse in unison, then pause to let individuals add their own thoughts and praises before continuing to the next.

    — After sharing, select a few verses of a praise psalm to paraphrase, building in the experiences of the group members that have been shared. Read as prayers several of these paraphrases, and use them at home during the week to praise the Lord.

    — Select praise verses from the Psalms for memorization by the group.

    — Discuss a psalm in depth, exploring the portrait of God it expresses and the works of God that have led to praise, relating all to our lives today.

— Write a modern-day psalm together, focusing it on a particular theme (God's goodness, power, some blessing).

32. *Testimony*

Address your sharing to the Lord, speaking directly to Him: "I praise You, Lord, for . . ." and continue to express something the Lord has done in your life the previous week.

33. *Spontaneous prayer*

Group members should be free to introduce prayer and praise to God at any time during the session. Spontaneous prayer may be of a short, interjectory nature — simply a "Thank You, Lord." Or a longer expression of praise and thanksgiving. Often groups will not develop this practice because it seems unusual (and thus uncomfortable for some) at first. Yet spontaneous prayers can help the group realize the immediate presence of the Lord — He *is* where the two or three are gathered! Spontaneous prayers can also help each person develop a sensitivity to the Lord's presence that will carry over into his daily life and lead to expressions of praise during the day and week.

To help the group feel comfortable in being involved in spontaneous prayer and praise experiences: (1) Talk over the whole idea as a group, thinking together of the values and discussing freely any hesitation members might have. (2) Plan to try spontaneous prayer for two sessions of the group meeting, encouraging members as they feel thankful to lead the group in expressing thanks right then. At first this will seem artificial — but it may lead to a truly spontaneous expression of worship and praise. (3) Select a praise leader for each session, asking him to keep sensitive to times when the group seems ready to praise the Lord or when it has shared experiences that naturally might lead to praise. After several weeks, no praise leader should be needed to keep the group aware of the Lord: all will be sensitized to His presence.

34. *Communion*

While some groups may feel that Communion should not be held without an ordained minister to lead, others have felt free to close a meeting with the breaking of bread. Communion is a joyful and yet solemn act of shared worship — an affirmation of Jesus as Savior and Lord and an evidence of commitment to Him until He comes again.

To hold Communion in a small group, read together (or appoint a member to read) 1 Cor. 11:23-28. Pass around a common loaf, from which each breaks a piece, and pass paper cups of juice. Prayer over the elements, and praise to the Lord, may be offered by members of the group as they will.

SESSION PLAN

The Bible study on pages 139-40 will lead your group into an experience of adoration.

7

additional resources

When a group of believers meets for ministry — and in the process develops a relationship in which each of the five essential elements of group life is present and in balance — personal and spiritual growth *does* take place.

Yet growing together as a group, and becoming the kind of group that experiences the relationships of the Body of Christ, is no automatic or easy task. Some groups do develop spontaneously and seem to grow quickly and easily into a biblical way of life. But others struggle and break down. Clearly, a special work of the Holy Spirit — welding believers together, opening hearts to love and be loved, quickening understanding to see and respond to the Lord — is vital and necessary.

What then can we do? Are we simply to come together and hope that the Lord will fashion us into a valid expression of His Body? Or can we come together and, depending fully on God's enablement for what happens with us, still seek to work with the Holy Spirit in those ways He has revealed in His Word?

This little book has been written in the conviction that the second option is open to us — and that we must take it. God has revealed His ways in His word just so that we might understand them and build our lives and our ways of living with each other firmly on His principles.

When we understand these areas, we have help in diagnosing the reasons why our groups might fall short of realizing their full potential. And we gain insight into how we can build our relationships toward that which God has planned for the members of His Church.

In this chapter, then, we will look at both *diagnostic* and *building* resources: suggestions for ways to understand what is happening in our groups, and for ways to deepen our experience of Identification, Affirmation, Exploration, Concentration, and Adoration. Use each of the following action resources when it seems appropriate in your group, or as suggested below.

ACTION IDEAS (Diagnostic)

(The numbering continues from the ACTION IDEAS on page 102.)

35. *Questionnaire*

    After the fourth or fifth meeting of the group, have each member complete the following questionnaire. Mark each statement with an *S* (I am generally satisfied with our progress and relationship), *U* (I am unsatisfied with our progress or relationship), or *D* (I have no feelings on this subject either way.)

    _____ (1) I am getting to know and appreciate others in our group.

    _____ (2) I feel free to express myself in the group.

    _____ (3) I feel others are expressing their real feelings and letting me come to know them in a meaningful way.

104

_____ (4) There is no individual or individuals with whom I am uncertain or by whom I some-times feel disliked.

_____ (5) I feel that most members of the group can and do understand me and the things I have to share.

_____ (6) I have felt really welcome in the group.

_____ (7) I have found it easy to express apprecia-tion and approval of others in the group.

_____ (8) I feel the others in the group really like and accept me.

_____ (9) I have actually told someone (in or after a group meeting) that I care about and am praying for him.

_____ (10) I have been told by members of the group that they care about and are praying for me.

_____ (11) I am learning things about God that I did not understand before.

_____ (12) I feel that our Bible studies are more than just a learning of information and they in-volve discovery of what the Word means for me.

_____ (13) I feel all members of the group are con-tributing to our understanding of what the Bible says and means to us.

_____ (14) I think the Bible is playing the role it ought to in our group.

_____ (15) I am satisfied with the methods and ap-proach to Bible study we are using now.

_____ (16) I sense an optimism in the group and an expectation that Christ will really work in us.

_____ (17) We are sharing meaningful things that the Lord is doing in our lives.

_____ (18) I am coming to realize how powerful and close Jesus is to me.

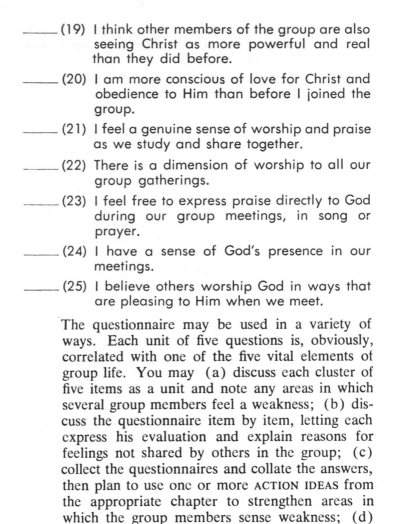

_____ (19) I think other members of the group are also seeing Christ as more powerful and real than they did before.

_____ (20) I am more conscious of love for Christ and obedience to Him than before I joined the group.

_____ (21) I feel a genuine sense of worship and praise as we study and share together.

_____ (22) There is a dimension of worship to all our group gatherings.

_____ (23) I feel free to express praise directly to God during our group meetings, in song or prayer.

_____ (24) I have a sense of God's presence in our meetings.

_____ (25) I believe others worship God in ways that are pleasing to Him when we meet.

The questionnaire may be used in a variety of ways. Each unit of five questions is, obviously, correlated with one of the five vital elements of group life. You may (a) discuss each cluster of five items as a unit and note any areas in which several group members feel a weakness; (b) discuss the questionnaire item by item, letting each express his evaluation and explain reasons for feelings not shared by others in the group; (c) collect the questionnaires and collate the answers, then plan to use one or more ACTION IDEAS from the appropriate chapter to strengthen areas in which the group members sense weakness; (d) locate interpersonal tensions by having each person add on the left the name or names of group members who seem to him the reason for an unsatisfactory experience on an item. This, too, may be collated and all the information given to every group member for discusison at the next meeting. Or, if an individual finds one name recurring on his questionnaire (a very likely occurrence), he

106

may be encouraged to get together with that person during the week to express his feelings and attempt to resolve the problem (cf. Matt. 5:23, 24).

36. *Group feedback*

After a number of weeks together, spend five sessions restudying the central chapters of this book (2-6). Have each member prepare by reading an agreed-on chapter and having ready some specific examples of ways that the group has included that element (Identification, Affirmation, Exploration, Concentration, or Adoration), or ways that a weakness in the area exists.

For group feedback to be effective, it is important that each person share honestly what he feels about the situation, and that each seek lovingly to help one another grow toward God's goal for His Body assembled.

37. *Paired feedback*

Sometimes it is easier for people to give feedback if they feel others share their perceptions. For paired feedback, give out the questionnaire (No. 35) but ask members of the group to meet in pairs before the next session to discuss their responses. When both members of a pair see a certain thing in the same light (either a strong positive or a strong negative), they covenant to share their feelings with the whole group at the next meeting.

38. *Individual feedback*

Give each group member a 3x5 or 4x6 card, one side of which is marked with a large plus (+), the other side of which is marked with a large minus (−). Each group member is to fill out each side of the card, completing the following statements.

+ *The greatest benefit of the group to me has been . . .*
and

*— My biggest disappointment about the group
has been . . .*

If an individual does not feel strongly about either
a plus or minus, he need not fill out that side of
the card.

When all are completed, begin at random and
have the first person read a plus, explaining why
he has written what he has. The next person,
moving to his right, then reads a minus, again
explaining why he has written what he has. Individuals may be questioned and their perceptions
discussed by the group.

Another way: all the pluses, or all the minuses,
may be read aloud, and then the feelings of the
whole group discussed as they have been revealed
in the report. Be sure to conclude such a session
with a discussion of steps to take to strengthen
the group and realize God's purpose in you.

ACTION IDEAS (Building)

One of the best ways to launch a group experience and get off to a balanced start is to plan a
week-end retreat. In this longer period of time,
group members can come to know each other rela-
tively well and also can work on some of the skills
that will help the group function effectively. This
group of ACTION IDEAS is put together to fashion a
retreat, run on the following schedule, for a Friday
night and Saturday period.

39. *The Retreat*

The retreat itself should involve all members of
newly formed groups and should plan to involve
eight to ten members who will be the nucleus of
a new group in experiences together. As many
groups as you wish may be formed and launched
on a single retreat, and if possible they should
only be launched in a retreat setting.

SCHEDULE NO. 1

FRIDAY			SATURDAY		
Arrival	6:30		Breakfast	7:30	
Settled in	7:00		Sharing (whole group)	8:00	**(42)**
Building acquaintance (8s)	7:05	**(40)**	Team creativity	9:00	**(43)**
Snack break	9:05		Sharing by teams	11:00	**(44)**
Studying together	9:25	**(41)**	Lunch	11:45	
Lights out	11:00		Studying together	1:00	**(45)**
			Sharing goals/worship	3:00	**(46)**
			Departure	4:15	

(The bold-faced numbers in the schedule correspond to the numbered items which follow on the next seventeen pages.)

40. *Building acquaintance*

The following pattern helps group members learn about each other, and it also helps individuals begin to reveal things about themselves in a non-threatening context. This initiation to self-revelation is very important.

- Place participants in the groups they will be with after the retreat. Then divide into pairs within each group. Each person is to tell his partner "all he needs to know" to understand him as a person — in three minutes. Then these roles are reversed.

- Next the small groups come together, and each person has 1½ minutes to help the group understand his partner as a person. Everyone is free to interject questions and comments, and the groups should be permitted to run over the suggested time limit.

- Each group member is then asked to check his perception of other members by saying what he thinks they were like at age seven. One of the group is selected as first subject. Each then shares his impression of the subject-person as a seven-year-old. The subject is then invited to tell what the group saw correctly and incorrectly. In the process, he begins to share more about himself. The process is then repeated with another person as subject.

- At this point each member is asked to recall himself at age seventeen and imagine this situation: *At seventeen I develop serious questions about my faith. How would I handle my doubts? Share them? With whom? Hide them? Suppress them?*

110

Why? Here, too, conversation within the group is encouraged, as each person begins to reveal how he tends to handle socially unacceptable thoughts and feelings.

- The retreat leader concludes this segment with a reading of 2 Corinthians 1:3-11, pointing out the importance of being ourselves and expressing ourselves if we are to minister to one another.

41. Groups meet together and do the following Bible study, adapted from a Serendipity study developed by Lyman Coleman. Each step is to be taken in sequence, with no looking ahead by members of the group. A properly folded sheet permits this kind of process to take place easily and naturally and at a pace set by the group members themselves. *The sketches and numbered exercises which follow explain the Bible study for No. 41.*

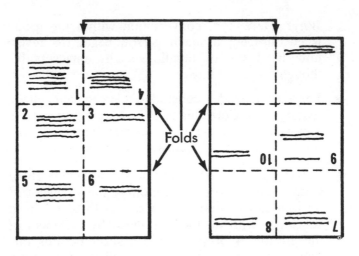

Figure 1	**Figure 2**
a. Fold 5 and 6 up behind 2 and 3. b. Fold 1 and 4 down and over 5 and 6. c. Fold 2 over 3.	This is the reverse side of the Bible study sheet before it is folded.

Figure 3

The Bible study sheet, when folded properly, looks like this and is ready to use.

1. Read the Bible passage in exercise 2. Think about the man described. What kind of person is he?

   Perhaps picture yourself as a psychiatrist, developing a case history. From what you see in the Bible text (the man's past, present associations, etc.), what kind of person would you say he was when Jesus first spoke to him?

   Turn to exercise 2, and spend 10-15 minutes developing your "case history."

2. Now there is in Jerusalem by the Sheep Gate a pool, in Hebrew called Beth-zatha, which has five porticoes. In these lay a multitude of invalids, blind, lame, paralyzed. One man was there, who had been ill for thirty-eight years. When Jesus saw him and knew that he had been lying there a long time, he said to him, "Do you want to be healed?" The sick man answered him, "Sir, I have no man to put me in the pool when the water is troubled, and while I am going another steps down before me." Jesus said to him, "Rise, take up your pallet, and walk" And at once the man was healed, and he took up his pallet and walked.

   (John 5:2-9 RSV)

3. Case history notes.

When done, turn together to exercise 4.

4. NOW, go around your group and let each share his insights.

Particularly, talk together about why Jesus might have asked, "Do you **want** to be healed?"

You do not have to agree, so don't try to win others to your understanding of the man. Simply explore the possibilities, share your ideas, and listen to each other.

Take up to 20 minutes. When finished, open the sheet to exercise 5.

5. Jesus is as real today as He was by Beth-zatha. He is just as able to heal and to transform. And we are in as great need as the sick man. Jesus asks us the same kind of probing, challenging question:

"Do you want to be healed?"

If Jesus were to ask you this question now, what in your life would He most likely be speaking of?

Take 3-5 minutes and jot down likely possibilities.

6. My own "infirmities"?

When all are done, move together to exercise 7, which is on the reverse side of the study sheet.

7. Now go around your circle and share the thing or things you pinpointed as personal needs or infirmities.

Take as long as you need to really understand what each person is sharing.

Then turn down the flap to do exercises 9 and 10 together.

8. Notes on what each shares.

9. Giving gifts.

When Jesus saw the need of the man by the pool, He gave him a gift that met his need.

What gift would you like to give each person in your group, in Jesus' name?

Think for a moment of what each has shared. Jot down a gift by his name that reveals what you believe Jesus wants to do for him. Then move around the circle, everyone giving your gifts to each person in turn.

10. The gifts I give . . . and receive.

When the gifts have been given, join hands and pray for each other as your time of community draws to a close.

42. All on the retreat share breakfast and, as devotions after the meal, each person shares a verse of Scripture and explains why that verse is important to him. Each person is limited to 30 seconds for his sharing.

43. *Team creativity*

Divide again into the functioning small groups (8s or 10s). If you are in a camp retreat setting, have group members use materials they can, find outdoors. If in a motel or other indoor setting, bring a variety of materials — paper, picture magazines, etc. Each group is to use the materials to create *together* a model or a poster of "God's work in our lives."

Encourage group members to spend at least a half hour talking together about how God works in persons, what He does, where He begins, what His goals are, how His work can be recognized. Then, working together, find ways to build a model or represent on a poster what the group has talked of, letting additional thoughts find creative expression as the project is being developed.

Stress that this is to be a team project: each person should feel that he makes a significant contribution to the creation of the whole.

44. *Team sharing*

When projects are completed, each small group should share with the whole group by showing and explaining its model or poster. This may be done by a designated individual, or each member of the team may be asked to explain a particular feature of the completed creation.

45. *God's creation*

Spend the afternoon studying in the small groups, using the same procedure as in No. 41 (page 111).

118

This particular study focuses on God's work of creation and the ways in which He shows by what He created (1) how important people are to Him and (2) how He communicates specialness to us.

The sketches and numbered diagrams which follow explain the Bible study on God's creation.

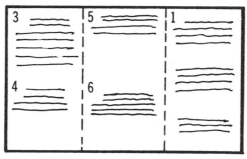

Figure 4

The Bible study sheet for No. 45 is folded accordion-style so that exercise 1 is visible.

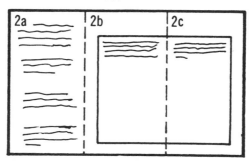

Figure 5

The reverse side of the study sheet shows exercise 2 and the chart panels accompanying it.

119

1

The Bible says only of man "God created man in his own image, in the image of God created he him; male and female created he them" (Gen. 1:27).

People were, and are, very special to God.

Jot down here one way that you feel you are special.

_____

_____

_____

_____

Record also one additional thing that you like about yourself — one other thing that makes you feel like a special and worthwhile person.

_____

_____

_____

_____

THEN

Share with one another (10-15 minutes) what you recorded before you turn to exercise 2.

2a

Read the following verses from Genesis 2 which show how God communicated to man that people are special to Him, and complete the chart panels. (Study individually for 10-15 minutes.)

7. And the Lord God formed man of the dust of the ground, and breathed into his nostrils the breath of life; and man became a living soul. 8. And the Lord God planted a garden eastward in Eden; and there he put the man whom he had formed. 9. And out of the ground made the Lord God to grow every tree that is pleasant to the sight, and good for food.

15. And the Lord God took the man, and put him into the garden of Eden to dress it and to keep it. 16. And the Lord God commanded the man, saying, Of every tree of the garden thou mayest freely eat: 17 But of the tree of the knowledge of good and evil, thou shalt not eat of it: for in the day that thou eatest thereof thou shalt surely die.

18. And the Lord God said, It is not good that the man should be alone; I will make him an help meet for him.

19. And out of the ground the Lord God formed every beast of the field, and every fowl of the air; and brought them unto Adam to see what he would call them: and whatsoever Adam called every living creature, that was the name thereof.

20b. But for Adam there was not found an help meet for him. 21. And the Lord God caused a deep sleep to fall upon Adam, and he slept: and he took one of his ribs, and closed up the flesh instead thereof; 22. And the rib, which the Lord God had taken from man, made he a woman, and brought her unto the man. 23. And Adam said, This is now bone of my bones, and flesh of my flesh.

2b

What need of man does God here recognize and act to meet?

2c

How does God's action here affirm that people are important to Him?

3

Select one of God's actions discovered in the study in exercise 2 which seems to you to communicate best a sense of God's love to you. Share with the group what this action is and why you chose it (15-20 minutes for all to share).

4

From what your group members have all shared above about how love is communicated to them, see if you can decide together on effective ways to help each other realize that each person is really special to God and worth loving by the group as well (20-30 minutes).

How we can communicate love

1.

2.

3.

4.

5.

6.

7.

8.

9.

10.

5

Affirm one another — communicate to each person that we appreciate him and see him as special to us.

From your time together, jot down the first name of each person in your group, and write one way in which he seems special to you. When all have finished, begin with one member of the group and, speaking directly to him, let each person say, "_____; I appreciate you because . . ."

Go around in this way with each group member (no time limit).

6

Close with prayer, thanking God for His love and for one another.

46. *Sharing goals/worship*

> Call everyone on the retreat together for closing worship. All join hands to form a linked circle, to share in an open time of prayer, telling the Lord why individuals came on this retreat and wanted to become members of a small group, and thanking him for progress toward the goal sensed on the weekend. Intersperse worship and praise choruses and songs with the prayer, and conclude by singing "They'll Know We Are Christians by Our Love."

A second retreat schedule for a longer weekend, focusing on Exploration and Concentration (as the first focuses on Identification and Affirmation), may also be used to launch the groups. Or, it might be used at a later time to strengthen and deepen relationships already initiated.

(The bold-faced numbers in the schedule correspond to the numbered items which follow on the next fourteen pages.)

SCHEDULE NO. 2

FRIDAY		SATURDAY		SUNDAY	
Arrival	6:30	Sleep in		Quiet time until	9:00
Snack/acquaintance	6:45 **(47)**	Open snack breakfast	8:30-9:30	Praise time	9:00 **(54)**
Self-portrait	7:15 **(48)**	Ideal self-portrait	9:30 **(50)**	Quaker meeting	10:00 **(55)**
Study John 14, 15	9:00 **(49)**	Study Acts 4:23-31	10:30 **(51)**	Choral praise	11:15 **(56)**
Singing	11:00	Lunch	12:30	Breakfast	11:30
		Activity/free time	1:30	Departure	12:30
		Supper	5:00		
		Strength recognition	6:00 **(52)**		
		Study Ephesians 3:13-21	9:15 **(53)**		
		Singing (optional)			

47. *Snack/acquaintance*

As participants arrive, tag each with a color for the group he is (or will be) in. Also pin on 8½x11 sheet of paper to each person's back. During snack time, each one is to find and talk to every member of his group, to discover one new fact about each person. This is then recorded on the individual's back. The next member of the group to talk to the individual has to add to the list another new item.

When the groups assemble, the members sit in a circle. Each person takes the list of the person on his right and reads it as an introduction of that individual to the group.

48. *Self-portrait*

Give each participant a large sheet of oaktag paper (or light poster board) and crayons. Each is to draw a design (using colors and shapes as he wishes) to represent himself, as he sees himself right now.

When completed, each shows his self-portrait to the group and explains his picture in detail. Questions may be asked by the group.

49. *Study John 14, 15 (Exploration)*

The sketches and numbered exercises which follow explain the Bible study on John 14, 15, which concludes the first evening.

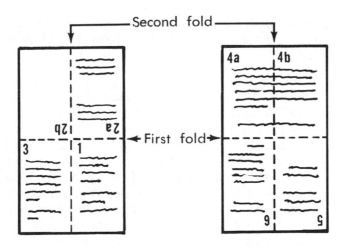

Figure 6

Fold paper as shown, with numbered exercises arranged this way.

Figure 7

Reverse side of paper has numbered items arranged as shown.

1. Before beginning the Bible study, think about the self-portraits we have just shared. List the most deeply felt needs that the sharing revealed.

_____
_____
_____
_____
_____
_____
_____
_____
_____

What is your most deeply felt need as you begin this weekend? What do you want most for God to do in your life?

_____
_____
_____

(5 minutes)

2a. Individually: paraphrase in the space on the right (2b) the following section of John 15 (15 minutes).

I am the true vine, and my Father is the vinedresser. Every branch of mine that bears no fruit, he takes away, and every branch that does bear fruit he prunes, that it may bear more fruit. You are already made clean by the word which I have spoken to you. Abide in me, and I in you. As the branch cannot bear fruit by itself, unless it abides in the vine, neither can you, unless you abide in me. I am the vine, you are the branches, He who abides in me, and I in him, he it is that bears much fruit, for apart from me you can do nothing (John 15:1-5 RSV).

From this paragraph, answer:

(1) What do you think "fruit" is? (See Gal. 5: 22.)

(2) What is "abiding?" How might we define it?

(3) Is the main thrust of this passage to warn or to promise? Why do you think so?

3. Together, discuss your answers to the questions and read aloud any sections of the paraphrases that seem particularly good or that you have questions about. (15-20 minutes).

THEN work together to see of you can define what it means to "abide" and what a person does to "abide in Christ." Key verses for your discussion: John 14:15, 21; 15:7, 9, 10. When you have come to an agreement, record your explanation in the space below (20- ? minutes).

4a and 4b. Read aloud the following passage from the book, *69 Ways to Start a Study Group and Keep It Growing,* page 89 and following.

"Love produces obedience. And in obedience the reality of God's presence is made plain.

"It shouldn't be hard to understand this. Sometimes we try to obey out of a sense of duty. Then obedience is a grudging struggle, an attempt to do what we feel God demands of us. But this is always doomed to failure. We're not able to do all we should. . . .

"But sometimes we're moved by love to obey. And what a different focus! Love doesn't think of itself; love fixes its eyes on the loved one. When this happens, we're aware of Jesus, and we discover in amazement that we have done what we could never do before! In forgetting ourselves and thinking of Jesus, we have moved from the *static* to the *dynamic* in life, and we actually experience the reality of Jesus' adequacy.

"There are two realities that we may experience. (1) The reality of our inadequacy. (2) The reality of Jesus' adequacy.

"When we concentrate on Jesus and love for Him, Jesus fulfills His promise that His disciples will 'keep my words.' In the actual doing of the word, which requires this divine enabling, we experience God's power. . . .

"Throughout the significant Upper Room chapters (John 13 - 17), this thought is emphasized and reemphasized. 'Abide in me,' Jesus encourages. 'Live close to me.' How? 'If you keep my commandments, you will abide in my love' (John 15:10 RSV)."

Abiding, or "staying close to Jesus," involves
(1) loving Him
(2) love-motivated (*not* duty-motivated) obedience
(3) experience of Jesus' enablement to live beyond ourselves.

(Take time to discuss the quote and the conclusions before moving on to exercise 5.)

5. Reread the John 15 passage again and together list: "What evidences can I see here of Jesus' love for me?" "What reasons can I find to love Him?" (Think together in depth.)

_____

_____

_____

_____

_____

_____

_____

_____

_____

6. Finally, turn again to exercise 1 and make a list containing all the items each member of the group listed on his own sheet. Then, beside each item, agree together on a "fruit" that the Lord promises to produce in us to replace the needs discovered.

End your time together by thanking the Lord that He is able to produce fruit, and that He promises to do just this in our lives as we love Him and live close to Him.

SATURDAY

50. *Ideal self-portrait*

Give out crayons and oaktag again, but this time ask each person to portray himself as he *wants* to be, that is, to portray his ideal self.

When complete, each person shows his portrait to his group and explains it.

51. *Study Acts 4:23-31* (Concentration)

Give out study guides for an exploration of Acts 4:23-31, which will help bring into focus God's power to help the participants realize the ideal. The sketches and numbered exercises which follow describe the study guide.

NOTE: Before distributing the study guides, have one person read aloud Acts 3:1-12 and 4:1-22 as background to the whole group.

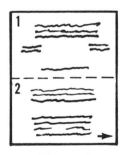

Figure 8
Fold sheet once so that only exercise 1 is visible.

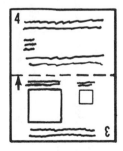

Figure 9
Reverse side shows how exercises 3 and 4 are arranged.

1

From your knowledge about Peter and John as they are portrayed in the Gospels, develop a list of **differences** and **similarities** between them and the Peter and John we see here in Acts. Work together for 15 to 20 minutes to do a careful analysis.

In the Gospels
(before the Resurrection)

In Acts
(after the Resurrection)

(Then turn down to exercise 2.)

2

Acts 4:23-31 records the response of Peter and John to the challenge. Read, and, individually UNDERLINE sections that reveal these men's image of God, and CIRCLE sections that reveal their image of themselves (5-8 minutes).

23 When they were released they went to their friends and reported what the chief priests and elders had said to them. 24 And when they heard it, they lifted their voices together to God and said, "Sovereign Lord, who didst make the heaven and the earth and the sea and everything in them, 25 who by the mouth of our father David, thy servant, didst say by the Holy Spirit, 'Why did the Gentiles rage, and the peoples imagine vain things? 26 The kings of the earth set themselves in array, and the rulers were gathered together, against the Lord and against his Anointed' — 27 for truly in this city there were gathered together against thy holy servant Jesus, whom thou didst anoint, both Herod and Pontius Pilate, with the Gentiles and the peoples of Israel, 28 to do whatever thy hand and thy plan had predestined to take place. 29 And now, Lord, look upon their threats and grant to thy servants to speak thy word with all boldness, 30 while thou stretchest out thy hand to heal, and signs and wonders are performed through the name of thy holy servant Jesus." 31 And when they had prayed, the place in which they were gathered together was shaken; and they were all filled with the Holy Spirit and spoke the word of God with boldness. (RSV)

(over)

3

Together, from your study, write in the boxes below words that seem to describe the disciples' view of themselves, and their view of the Lord (15-20 minutes).

John and Peter saw themselves as . . .

John and Peter saw God as . . .

4

Complete together:

1. John and Peter were realistic about . . .

2. What seemed most important to John and Peter was not their _____ but God's _____.

3. John and Peter responded to the challenge to them to live beyond themselves by . . .

    (a)

    (b)

    (c)

    (d)

    (?)

4. The result of their approach to their need for courage and boldness was . . .

    Now, together . . .

Apply Principles Seen in This Passage to Your Own Lives and Awareness of Needs as Seen in the Gap Between Your Ideal Self and Who You Are Now. That is, take five minutes to meditate on **what does this mean for me** . . . and then share your specific applications with the other members of your small group.

52. *Strength recognition exercise*

Tape to the wall large sheets of newsprint, one for each member of a small group. Give each person a felt-tipped pen. On his sheet a person is to record, beginning with childhood, every "success" he can remember. Take up to thirty minutes for this part of this activity.

When everyone is finished, one member sits near the center of the group, and all the others examine what he has recorded on his sheet. The group is to examine the recorded successes and discuss, while the subject remains silent: (1) What constitutes success for _____? [For some, it may be personal or artistic achievement, sports, making money, or friendship development.] (2) What strengths does the chart reveal _____? (3) What possible warnings or dangers are indicated?

After the group has discussed, the person may respond if he wishes. Then another member of the group shows his list, and the process is repeated.

When this activity is completed, the group should be reminded, "God has made each of us special, with our own unique gifts and talents. But we can't depend on these abilities alone; Even our strengths may become weaknesses. Yet Christ's power is available to flow through us and vitalize every strength and talent for His glory and for the benefit of other people."

The group may pause for prayer or move directly to the next Bible study.

53. *Study Ephesians 3:14-21* (Adoration)

138

1. Meditate on this prayer, then record your insights along each margin. (20 minutes)

In my own words . . .	A prayer for ME	In my own words . . .
What does God want and intend to do for me?	That he [the Father of our Lord Jesus Christ] would grant you, according to the riches of his glory, to be strengthened with might by his Spirit in the inner man; That Christ may dwell in your hearts by faith; that ye, being rooted and grounded in love, May be able to comprehend with all saints what is the breadth, and length, and depth, and height; And to know the love of Christ, which passeth knowledge, that ye might be filled with all the fulness of God.	How can I be sure He will do this in me?

(record here)	Now unto him that is able to do
	       exceeding
	        abundantly
	    above all that we ask
	      or think,
	
	according to the power that worketh in us, Unto him be glory in the church by Christ Jesus throughout all ages, world without end. Amen. **Ephesians 3:16-21**
		(record here)

2. How can you express your praise to God? (30-45 minutes)

Select one verse or phrase from the Scripture passage that is most meaningful to you, and express your praise in one of the following ways, or in some other creative way:

   a. Make a poster.
   b. Write your own psalm.
   c. Write a chorus or a song to sing.
   d. Write a prayer poem.
   e. Plan a pantomime.
   f. Find a hymn that expresses your feelings.
   g. Draw or paint a picture.

3. Come together for a worship time. (30-60 minutes)

Let each person share what was most meaningful to him in the passage, and why, then use what he has created to lead the others in worship of the Lord.

Serve coffee but no breakfast, and have no one speak to another person but meditate in silence until the meeting at nine.

54. *Praise time*

Organize praise time around two themes, expressed both in spontaneously begun songs and vocalized prayers and praise. The themes, which may be set by two posters, are

Let us praise God for who He is
Let us praise God for what He has
done in us

55. *Quaker meeting*

Let everyone know Saturday night that they will have the opportunity on Sunday morning to share from their quiet time and learnings of the week. You may want to ask two or three to prepare longer, ten-minute studies or devotionals around the theme of the weekend. But the meeting should be open for all to participate in, to share from Scripture, to encourage, rebuke, exhort, teach, or testify.

56. *Choral praise*

Conclude the time of worship by dividing into two equal groups, to read alternately the verses of Psalm 136, which praises God and recalls His steadfast lovingkindness.

PUBLISHED RESOURCES

The following list suggests additional published resources that give insights and ideas into the small group or that may be used to guide small group sessions.

57. *Relational Bible studies*

A number of Serendipity study books have been written by Lyman Coleman and are published by

Word, Inc., 4800 West Waco Drive, Waco, Texas 76703. Some of these studies are excellent and hold a rich fund of ideas along with well-planned guides to small group interaction.

58. *Growth-by-Groups*

An earlier approach developed by Coleman, these study guides focus on the study and application of Scripture, with each group member responsible to prepare by study and living for the group meetings. A solid, helpful approach, available from Huntington Park, Virginia.

59. *Group ideas*

The magazine *Faith at Work* includes helpful ideas for groups in a regular feature. You may subscribe by writing in care of Faith at Work, 295 Madison Avenue, New York, NY 10017.

60. *Simulation games*

Various activities designed for exploring interpersonal and communications problems have been developed under this title. A variety of games in a Christian framework and a bibliography of organizations supplying simulation materials are available from Richard C. Muzik, 803 E. Grand River, East Lansing, Michigan 48823. Phone: (517) 351-4260.

61. *Small groups in the church*

A discussion and exploration of the role of the small group in the local church is contained in this author's book, *A New Face for the Church* (Zondervan, 1970). An example of how principles explored in *New Face* are put into action is provided in Robert C. Girard's book, *Brethren, Hang Loose* (Zondervan, 1972), which shares how the church he pastors has been restructured around small groups.

62. *The nature of unity*

A book that explores the nature of the Christian's unity with other believers and has a study guide adapting it for use by classes or small ministry groups is *Becoming One in the Spirit* by this author (Scripture Press/Pyramid).

63. *Interpersonal openness and honesty*

Books that might be used by a study group to help members learn to share openly and build identity with one another are Keith Miller's *Taste of New Wine* (Word Books, 1965; study guide available) and Bruce Larson's *Living on the Growing Edge* (Zondervan, 1968).

64. *An achievement motivation approach*

A distinctive approach to relationship-building, developed by some Christian men, communicates theory and suggests a variety of group experiences. You can find out what they have available by writing to

Achievement Motivation Program Headquarters
1439 S. Michigan Ave.
Chicago, Illinois 60605
Phone: (312) 427-2500

65. *Group training*

Each spring in early June the author holds a ten-day seminar on "The Ministry of the Layman" at Honey Rock Camp, Three Lakes, Wisconsin. This seminar, offering undergraduate or graduate credit through Wheaton College, Wheaton, Illinois, involves experience of small group dynamics and training in building laymen in the local church for ministry through ministry groups. For information on dates and costs, write to Christian Ministries Department, Graduate School, Wheaton College, Wheaton, Illinois 60187. The seminar is open to a limited number of ministers and laymen each year.

66. *Songs*

The following books provide sources for contemporary choruses and songs that might be used in small group worship and praise: *Crowning Glory Hymnal* (Grand Rapids: Singspiration, Inc.); *Folk Hymnal* (Singspiration); *Praise Hymnal* (Singspiration).

67. *Research*

An organization that explores the role of the small group in the local church, and other facets of church renewal, publishes a newsletter called *interCHANGE*. It is available by subscription from:

Renewal Research Associates
14411 N. 6th Street
Phoenix, Arizona 85022

68. *Bible versions*

Keep the group members thinking together by using the same versions of the Bible for study, but referring to additional ones for paraphrasing. The best versions, selected because of their accuracy and careful correspondence to the original texts are: as a translation, the *New International Version;* as a paraphrase of the New Testament, *Phillips* [*The New Testament in Modern English* by J. B. Phillips].

69. *Various kinds of groups*

For insights into various kinds of groups and how they function, see one of the following books: *Small Group Ministry in the Contemporary Church* (Herald House); *Growth Through Groups* (Broadman Press); *Team Building in Church Groups* (Judson Press); *Sharing Groups in the Church* (Abingdon Press).